PARANORMAL STORIES

Supernatural Tales and Unexplained Mysteries from Across the World

JAMIE KING

summersdale

DISCLAIMER

By their very nature, paranormal stories come in all shapes and sizes. The author and the publishers make no claim that any of these stories have any basis in fact. They are merely tales that have enjoyed popularity in the public domain in some form or another. Such stories are reproduced herein for entertainment purposes only and are not intended to be taken literally.

PARANORMAL STORIES

PARANORMAL STORIES

Copyright © Summersdale Publishers Ltd, 2022

Text by Emily Kearns

An Hachette UK Company
www.hachette.co.uk

Summersdale Publishers Ltd
Part of Octopus Publishing Group Limited
Carmelite House
50 Victoria Embankment
LONDON
EC4Y 0DZ
UK

www.summersdale.com

Printed and bound by CPI Group (UK) Ltd, Croydon, CR0 4YY

ISBN: 978-1-80007-189-6

Substantial discounts on bulk quantities of Summersdale books are available to corporations, professional associations and other organizations. For details contact general enquiries: telephone: +44 (0) 1243 771107 or email: enquiries@summersdale.com.

CONTENTS

INTRODUCTION

Take a moment, if you will, to open your mind to the unusual. We all love science – that wonderful and progressive thing that explains the world to us – but sometimes even science is stumped. You just can't explain the unexplainable.

Over the following pages you'll find yourself immersed in a world of paranormal possibilities. These tales are rooted in myth and legend with accounts from eyewitnesses who say these things really happened, these creatures and entities really exist – but it's up to you to make up your own mind, we're just here to tell the stories.

Set off on a journey taking in spectres and spooks and some of the most terrifyingly haunted buildings in the world. From ghostly impressions of historical figures, left behind on Earth with their unresolved issues, to those taken too soon and whose phantoms aren't yet ready to cross over to the next world. Meet the demons that lurk where you least expect them, or those that reside within us, and the poltergeists that terrorize families for years on end.

Take in the history of those who sparked a huge movement by contacting spirits on the other side, the way this changed contemporary society and the notable figures who bought into it all in a big way. Meet the magicians and tricksters, practitioners of black magic and the dark arts, and the innocents who got swept up in the commotion.

Open up to the realms of cryptozoology and the possibilities of creatures we know little about, from Bigfoot to Mothman, death worms, jackalopes, kelpies, swamp monsters, the Minotaur and everything in between. Stepping away from cryptids, there are the blood-drinkers, the moon-howlers and the flesh-eaters – the crowd-pleasers and show-stealers of any round-up of paranormal creatures.

Reminisce about Roswell, crop circles and alien abduction, not to mention strange lights in the sky all over the world and throughout history claiming to explain whether we have intelligent company in this universe of ours. Then, finally, experience the mysteries of time travel through the stories of others; and the curious tales of glitches in the matrix and steps into alternate realities where doppelgängers tap into one universe from another.

It's a wild ride – so buckle up.

GHOSTS AND HAUNTINGS

From lost souls cursed to roam the Earth for eternity, to those seeking vengeance in the living world and others craving a human touch just out of reach, spectral experiences are by far the most widely reported of all paranormal activity.

Ghost stories have featured heavily in history since ancient times – in various religions, secular traditions, entertainment and healing – although today we might be more familiar with ghost-hunters and pseudoscientists on TV, as well as sensationalized tales in the media.

Ghosts are classified as visions of the dead who often make themselves seen by the living. When it comes to poltergeists, however, many believe them to be more of a kinetic energy presence that causes physical disturbances – there is definitely crossover with the ghost world, but we'll deal with those pesky poltergeists in the next chapter. It's generally believed that ghosts are unable to break through into the physical world in this way, but they nearly always have unresolved issues and rarely stray from where they lived as mortals.

There's the subtle – the mere feeling of a presence to faraway footsteps or the flicker of a candle – and then the full-on, no-holds-barred visual extravaganza of a ghostly spectacle, perhaps floating but more often simply wandering down a dimly lit corridor. In this chapter we'll visit a ghost town where disturbed graves have disrupted weary souls, abandoned hospitals where the dead don't rest and a hotel where the local spook might give you a gentle embrace if you're lucky – or unlucky – enough.

From the most haunted pub in London to the most haunted forest in Japan; lighthouses inhabited by ghost children longing to play hide and seek, and prisons that have seen such unspeakable things done to humans that their spirits choose to remain despite their bodies leaving this world. Prep your spine for a good chilling, because it's all here.

HAUNTINGS OF HAMPTON COURT

Best known as the residence of notorious serial marrier King Henry VIII, Hampton Court Palace in Surrey has long been considered one of the most haunted stately homes in England. With a penchant for divorcing and beheading wives who didn't quite live up to his high standards, there could indeed be good reason for miffed spirits to hang around.

Many people believe at least two of Henry's ex-wives haunt the palace and plenty of witnesses have come forward to back this up. A pale and sad-looking ghostly figure carrying a lighted taper is said to be Jane Seymour, Henry's third wife, who died shortly after giving birth to his son, who became the boy king Edward VI. The pale figure has been seen numerous times on the Silverstick Stairs – which once led to the room in which Jane Seymour gave birth and died – on the anniversary of Edward's birth. In the 1920s, an enterprising caretaker supposedly took photographs of her ghost and sold them to tourists.

The ghost of Henry's fifth wife, Catherine Howard, whom he had beheaded for alleged adultery and treason, is seen even more often and is allegedly far more vocal. So the story goes,

Catherine was arrested at Hampton Court Palace but was able to break away from the guards, running down what is now referred to as the Haunted Gallery and screaming out to Henry for mercy. The guards recaptured her and she never saw the king again. She was executed at the Tower of London, aged only 19. Sightings of her heartbroken, anguished ghost repeating her desperate pleas through the gallery have regularly been reported.

Besides the lingering distress of Henry's wives, there has been much talk of a ghostly "grey lady", whom many believe to be Sybil Penn – nurse to Elizabeth I and Edward VI. As a loyal family servant, when she caught smallpox from Elizabeth and died as a result, she was buried in the nearby church. Following church renovations, her tomb was disturbed in 1829 and after this the sightings began of a grey lady walking the corridors of the state apartments and clock court inside the palace.

Around 1871 a palace resident complained of a constant banging and knocking on her walls, but no one believed her. Not long after, two male skeletons were discovered in shallow graves close to her apartment. Once the bodies were given a proper burial, the racket stopped, much to the resident's relief. One theory is these unfortunates were murdered during the civil wars, buried in unmarked graves and concealed when the "baroque palace" was built on top of them by Sir Christopher Wren in 1689.

In October 2003 someone or something made a remarkable entrance at the palace. A set of fire doors were flung open on three consecutive days and on the second day a ghostly figure, dressed in a hooded robe, emerged before closing the doors again. The appearance was clearly captured on CCTV and can be viewed online. Security staff were both spooked and baffled at the appearance and remain so to this day, with no explanation as to who it was or how it occurred.

NORDIC NOIR

Akershus Fortress sits by the water in Norway's capital Oslo. It's considered to be so haunted that the locals take great pride in its paranormal prowess. Built in the 1300s, the place is ripe for spectral activity, with plenty of figures from history who might want to hang around. As well as serving as residence to royalty and political leaders, Akershus has also been used as a military base and prison over the centuries.

A woman with no face has been seen walking the halls; she wears a long robe and apparently emerges from the darkness to show herself to visitors. Sightings of ghostly castle guards have also been reported along with faces that appear in any fire that is lit in or around the castle, allegedly cackling and grinning maniacally.

Perhaps the most intriguing – and terrifying – of the paranormal activity at Akershus is that of the ghost dog that guards the castle gates. Legend has it that since the dog was buried alive its spirit continues to lurk and that anyone it approaches will die within the following three months.

PRISON PRESENCE

Eastern State Penitentiary in Philadelphia, Pennsylvania, is one of the most haunted buildings in the USA. Built in 1829, the medieval-castle-like prison building looms, casting a shadow over the road. This particular facility took solitary confinement to new levels, with prisoners doomed to exist alone – exercising, eating and living with no one but themselves for company. If a prisoner had to leave their cell, a hood would be placed over their head so they couldn't see or be seen. The authorities claimed that this system of solitary confinement would reform inmates and was more humane than the alternative. However, when Charles Dickens visited the prison in 1842 he disagreed with the method: "I hold this slow and daily tampering with the mysteries of the brain to be immeasurably worse than any torture of the body."

The extremes of solitary confinement were abandoned in 1913 due to overcrowding of the prison, but its severe forms of punishment continued in new guises (one inmate had his tongue chained to his wrists). In winter, inmates were dunked in a bath before being hung on a wall until ice formed on their skin. There was a chair in which prisoners were so tightly bound that their circulation was often cut off, leading to many amputations, and inmates could also be sent to "the hole" – a damp underground cell where captives were left to rot.

However, in 1929 Al Capone famously spent eight months in Eastern State and somehow managed to furnish his cell with oriental rugs, fine furniture and a radio. Capone's stay at Eastern State was his first stint in prison – some six years before his infamous incarceration at Alcatraz. He was travelling through Philadelphia, on his way between Atlantic City and his Chicago home, when he was stopped and arrested for carrying an unlicensed revolver. The authorities were keen to crack down on Capone, who was by this point a notorious bootlegger, and handed him the maximum sentence for the crime. As one might suspect, his reputation preceded him and the famous mob boss was treated exceedingly well by the (likely terrified) staff at Eastern State, making him far more comfortable than any other inmate.

With a history rife with murder, torture, suicide, madness and disease, it's little wonder there have been many, many reports of paranormal activity here – the troubled souls of former prisoners left to walk the crumbling, peeling cell blocks.

The prison closed in 1971 and was left to fall into ruin until the 1990s. With its grand, but gloomy stone fortress façade, the building was deemed worthy of preservation, restored and turned into a tourist attraction. If those walls could talk. The stories told by the staff that work the corridors are hair-raising. Cell block 12 is where staff and visitors have heard echoing voices and cackling, while cell block 6 is known for shadowy figures darting across the walls and pacing footsteps, and cell block 4 for the appearance of ghostly faces. One maintenance worker reported opening an old cell door lock when he felt a force grip him and hold on so tightly that he could not move.

He felt what he described as a horrible, negative energy forcing its way out of the cell and reported seeing tortured faces appear on the cell walls.

Until recently, supernatural and crime history fans would flock in their thousands to Eastern State every year, to visit the museum and take part in the annual Terror Behind the Walls celebration every Halloween. Actors would assume the roles of prisoners to create a frightening display that was "as scary as possible", alongside attractions such as "zombie mud runs" and escape rooms. The horror show was deemed by many to be "too scary", and in more recent times has been toned down and much of it cleared to make way for a beer garden. But considering its placement in what is widely considered to be one of the most haunted spaces in America – would you dare to drink there?

HOSPITAL HAUNTING

The Old Changi Hospital in Singapore is purportedly home to a host of hauntings – hardly surprising when its history is so grisly. Built in 1935 as part of a military base, the hospital was used during the Japanese occupation as a merciless prison by the Kempeitai, the Japanese secret police. Many were tortured and killed there until the building became a hospital again at the end of the Second World War.

A new hospital was built on a different site in 1997 and Old Changi has been derelict ever since. Only the bravest enter the abandoned buildings, which are said to be alight with ghostly activity, haunted as they are by their bloody past. Sightings of bloodied Japanese soldiers, supposedly those who were executed here, and patients who never left, have been reported. The ghosts of those who died young are said to haunt the children's ward and loud bangs, crashes and screams have been heard by many a visitor.

HORROR HOUSE

Thought by many to be perhaps the most haunted house in the world, 112 Ocean Avenue in Amityville, New York state, has good reason to claim that chilling title. Owners past and present have done all they can to transform the building from its previous state in a bid to escape its bloody history. The famous quarter-moon windows have been replaced and the house number changed to deter spooky thrill seekers, so the infamous address of 112 Ocean Avenue no longer exists in this part of America. In more recent years the various owners of the house claim to have experienced precisely zero paranormal encounters – but of course they would say that.

In 1974, a 23-year-old man shot and killed his mother, father and four siblings in their house at 112 Ocean Avenue. At first, the man claimed it had been a mob killing but police quickly found holes in his version of events and it wasn't long before he confessed to the murders. He pleaded insanity, that he killed his family because he had heard their voices plotting against him, and was incarcerated until his death in 2021. Following his conviction, he lied incessantly about what had happened that night, offering several different stories as to who had carried out the murders – at one point implicating his mother. Police were also baffled that none of the neighbours on Ocean

Avenue reported hearing gunshots, despite the murder weapon being a rifle with no silencer. All they heard was the family dog barking at around the same time.

Following the murders and the trial, a new family moved into the house, which was priced incredibly cheaply, for obvious reasons, but the new owners were unaware of its history when they bought it. Much of the deceased family's furniture came with the house and within a month things became very strange and frightening for the new residents. The house attracted great swarms of flies, doors were ripped from their hinges by a malicious presence and the family believed that the furniture had moved around on its own. On top of that there was continual banging on the doors and walls, cabinets slammed shut on their own, faces appeared around the house and green and black slime was said to ooze from the ceilings.

They eventually learned of the house's grisly past and arranged for a priest to carry out a blessing on the property. As the priest was blessing each room, he encountered a presence in one – a male voice telling him sternly to "get out". The next day the priest developed a fever and blisters, akin to stigmata, appeared on his hands.

The new family only stayed in the house for around four weeks, until one night of terrifying paranormal events led the residents to leave right away; the experiences were so frightening they even had difficulty talking about them. They never returned to the house and arranged for their possessions to be packed and moved. They sold their story to writer Jay Anson, who in 1977 published the bestseller *The Amityville Horror: A True Story*. A film franchise quickly followed, making the story of 112 Ocean Avenue one of the most discussed in spooky circles.

CLOVER THE FRIENDLY GHOST

The Hay-Adams Hotel in Washington DC has received a fair amount of attention in recent years thanks to its resident friendly phantom. A luxury affair, upon opening in 1928 the hotel went on to host celebrities of the age such as Charles Lindbergh and Amelia Earhart.

Many claim the hotel is haunted by Clover Adams, who was a socialite and the wife of writer Henry Adams – and possibly even the inspiration for Henry James' celebrated novel *The Portrait of a Lady*. In the 1870s, along with neighbours John Hay (who had been private secretary to Abraham Lincoln) and his wife Clara, the two couples were very much part of the Washington DC elite, moving in social circles with everyone from Teddy Roosevelt to Mark Twain.

The story goes that Clover – a passionate photographer – fell into a deep depression following the death of her father and took her own life by ingesting the potassium cyanide she used to develop film. The house in which she died was eventually ripped down, along with the house once owned by the Hays, and the hotel was built in its place.

GHOSTS AND HAUNTINGS

Guests to the hotel have encountered a ghostly figure on two of its floors, light switches turning on and off, and doors locking and unlocking of their own accord. Startlingly, housekeeping staff have reported the feeling of phantom arms wrapping them in an embrace.

RUMBLES ON THE UNDERGROUND

The London Underground has many ghostly goings-on beneath the surface and more than a few sad tales to tell.

During the Second World War many of the stations were used as civilian air-raid shelters and, while many lives were no doubt saved, this brought about new tragic incidents below ground.

East of Bethnal Green station that purportedly sheltered hundreds of locals from the war crowds began streaming toward the station to take cover during an air raid. Upon hearing a loud explosion (actually the testing of anti-aircraft weapons in nearby Victoria Park), panic ensued and many began pushing harder to get into the station. Near the bottom of the stairwell someone tripped and fell, causing a pile-up of 300 people. Casualties were many – mainly women and children – with 173 lives lost. There have been numerous reports from tube staff over the years of the sounds of children crying and women screaming echoing around the station after dark.

Elsewhere on the London Underground, in the latter half of the twentieth century, workers at Aldgate claim to have experienced an otherworldly presence down on the tracks.

Late one night, some years after the war was over, a worker fell on to the live rail and was electrocuted, with 20,000 volts shooting through his body. He survived but was knocked unconscious. When he came to, his fellow track workers said they had seen a ghostly figure of a woman stroking his hair just before he fell. She is thought to have been an apparition of a woman who was electrocuted and died in that station during the Second World War.

Over in Covent Garden a Victorian actor still puts on a show for station staff. Murdered at the stage door of the nearby Adelphi Theatre in 1897, William Terris – a "Hero of the Adelphi melodramas" according to his plaque at the venue – supposedly roams the platforms and tunnels at the station. There have been sightings of a tall, ghostly gentleman in Victorian dress and white gloves, and complaints of knocking sounds and light switches flicking on and off.

Across the pond, the New York Subway boasts hauntings of the highest order. At Astor Place, a spectral train has been seen arriving at the station. Witnesses claim to have caught a glimpse inside of lavish interiors, furnished with leather sofas, silk curtains and a wood-burning stove – descriptions bearing an uncanny resemblance to the private train carriage of August Belmont Jr, who financed the construction of the subway in the early 1900s. If that wasn't enough, President Franklin D. Roosevelt's trusty Scottish terrier Fala is said to wander the halls of Grand Central, searching for his master who had his own secret train platform just below the Waldorf Astoria hotel.

BEWARE ROOM 333

The Langham Hotel in London's upmarket Fitzrovia offers five-star luxury – as well as five-star spectral activity. Since the Langham's inception in 1865, Oscar Wilde, Mark Twain and Sir Arthur Conan Doyle have stayed there and that's just the tip of the celebrity iceberg.

Ghostly goings-on at the hotel are numerous and most seem to take place in one particularly haunted room. During October, room 333 regularly presents a Victorian doctor thought to have murdered his wife while on honeymoon before killing himself. The room has also seen numerous cameos by the ghost of a German prince in military dress, who they say threw himself from a window of the hotel on the fourth floor.

Terrifyingly, there is a also ghostly presence who has a penchant for shaking guests out of their beds at night; one occurrence of this in room 333 ended with the victim fleeing the hotel in the dead of night. Phantom hotel staff have also been spotted, still in service long after their souls have departed. There have also been reports of a man with a gaping wound in his face wandering the halls and areas of the hotel that felt strangely freezing cold.

FRIGHT IN THE FOREST

Japan's Aokigahara forest sits north-west of Mount Fuji and sprawls over 35 sq km (13.5 sq miles). The forest is so thick with foliage, it's also known as the "sea of trees" and it has been the backdrop for spooky films including 2016's aptly titled *The Forest*.

Aokigahara's other nickname is the "suicide forest", named for the devastating number of visitors who have entered and never left. As many as one hundred people kill themselves amid the trees every year. In a dark turn some claim this practice has been popularized by Seicho Matsumoto's 1960 novel *Kuroi Jukai*, in which a heartbroken lover chooses to end her life in Aoikighara.

The twisted trees of the forest are so densely packed there is little room for wind to travel through; and as there is hardly any wildlife to speak of, it is eerily quiet among the branches. Visitors have recounted their feeling of unease at the stillness among the trees and the absence of sound. Sitting at the base of a mountain, the area is littered with cave openings and the forest floor is rocky while the soil beneath is rich with iron, supposedly playing havoc with GPS systems and phone signals. Some believe this is demons at work and advise marking your way with ribbon or tape to ensure your escape from the thick, unforgiving forest. However, discoveries of deliberately cut tape, causing wanderers to lose their way, are thought to be the work of these demons.

Many believe the mournful spirits of the dead, claimed by the forest, still linger among the trees. Japanese folklore suggests these vengeful spirits are liable to lure sad, lonely visitors deep into the forest away from the path. One journalist who visited the forest recalled hearing a blood-curdling scream and hurriedly followed the sound only to find the body of a man who had been dead for some time. Other witnesses claim to have seen white figures drifting between the trees, some allegedly having been caught on camera.

Suicide is so common here that since the early 1970s volunteers have patrolled the area in order to recover remains and return them to the world beyond the forest to be laid to rest.

Should you enter the forest, you are sternly advised to stick to the paths. Grisly discoveries in the thick of the woods – such as clothing and personal belongings abandoned and claimed by nature, human bones and remains hanging from trees or strewn across the forest floor – suggest this is a place in which tourists should proceed with caution.

ISLAND GHOSTS

Just outside Venice in the lagoon on the way to Lido sits a small island. Poveglia is thought to have been inhabited as far back as 421 and remained so until 1379 when residents fled due to war. In the late 1700s, the main island building was used to quarantine plague sufferers, many of whom perished, their bodies burned on giant pyres. By the 1800s the building was in use as an asylum, where supposedly human experimentation took place and a doctor is believed to have jumped to his death from the bell tower.

The island has been abandoned since the 1970s and locals make a concerted effort to steer clear of it. Few dare set foot on Poveglia and those who fish the nearby waters refuse to get too close to the island, for fear of dredging up bodies.

Many who have been brave enough to visit have reported hearing voices and screams and seeing ghostly shadows dancing on the walls. Visitors have claimed they have become possessed while on the island, with one recounting overwhelming feelings of rage and another noting what they described as an oppressive evil feeling. It seems that, in the minds of many locals, Poveglia's grim history of disease, torture and suicide lingers on in the present.

WAILING WOMAN OF MEXICO CITY

The district of Xochimilco in southern Mexico City features a sizable network of canals, the last remnants of a vast water transport system built by the Aztecs.

Known as the "floating gardens of Mexico City", the waterways harbour more than a couple of ethereal residents, the most famous being the wailing woman or La Llorona. Legend has it that Maria, the wailer in question, caught her husband cheating on her and took revenge on him by drowning their two children in the canal. She immediately regretted her act but was unable to save them and, consumed by guilt, drowned herself. However, due to her murderous actions she was unable to cross over into the afterlife and instead doomed to roam the Earth for eternity, plagued by perpetual grief.

Sightings of a weeping, wailing woman, soaking wet and dressed in white, have been oft reported, with witnesses saying she cries out for her children. In a darker turn, some say she snatches young children from the waterfront as she walks, perhaps mistaking them for her own.

The story of La Llorona is deeply rooted in Mexican popular culture and is told to children to encourage them not to go out after dark, wander away from their parents or play close to dangerous water. The legend has been referenced in many works of literature, theatre, film and music, and a theatrical production of the story is performed on the waterfront in Xochimilco every year on November 1, the Day of the Dead or *Día de los Muertos*.

The wailing woman aside, these waters are also said to be home to *nahuales* – human spirits that have taken on animal form, often to perform magic or inflict harm on others – with reports of black, jaguar-like creatures swimming underneath boats only to jump on to the riverbank and bound into the woods.

Among the waterways lies the hauntingly macabre Island of Dolls, or *Isla de la Muñecas*, where grubby dolls in various stages of decapitation and mutilation hang from the trees. The story goes that a young girl drowned there and the man who discovered her body later found a doll in the water where the body had been. As a mark of respect, he strung up the doll from a tree on the island. However, the man felt haunted by the spirit of the drowned girl and so strung up more dolls in a bid to please her. She became increasingly demanding and one day the man was found dead in the water, floating in the spot where the girl's body had been found. Today, hundreds of dolls swing from the trees and shrieks of disembodied laughter have been reported by many an unsettled tourist.

SWEDISH SPIRITS

Standing since 1876, the humble Borgvattnet vicarage in Sweden is considered one of the spookiest buildings in the country. Since the late 1920s strange occurrences have been reported at the house and as one vicar and their family would move on, so the next vicar and their family would claim they had been subject to a variety of supernatural encounters.

Residents and visitors have heard disembodied screams and encountered ghostly shadow people, while washing has apparently been ripped from the line and objects moved around. Perhaps most terrifying of all are testimonies that an old, unoccupied rocking chair just kept on rocking of its own spooky volition.

Explanations range from mistreated servants returning to enact their revenge, to resident vicars of days gone by watching over the new residents. In the 1980s a man of the cloth calling himself the Ghost Priest attempted an exorcism of the house but as the spectral activity continued one can only say he was unsuccessful. The vicarage now operates as a B&B – are you brave enough to spend the night there?

TERROR IN THE TEN BELLS

The Ten Bells pub in London's East End is regarded as by far the most haunted hostelry in the capital. Built in the 1740s, it has associations with Jack the Ripper's murders, among other horrors.

The Ten Bells plays an important part in the Jack the Ripper story: his second victim Annie Chapman was said to have been drinking alone in the pub only hours before her body was discovered; his third victim Elizabeth Stride was also known to frequent the Ten Bells; and final victim Mary Kelly was seen there with a friend the night before her murder. Several of the Ripper's casualties were discovered close to the Ten Bells, only adding to the grisly history of the establishment.

Over the years, staff living above the pub claimed to spy a man in Victorian garb appearing and disappearing in the hallway, while others have complained of waking in the night feeling uneasy and turning over to find him lying next to them in their bed. At least he would disappear when they called out. Regular sightings of this ghostly figure are still being reported by customers and staff to this day. His identity remained a mystery until 2000 when a box was discovered in the cellar that contained items belonging to an ex-landlord of the Ten

Bells, who was allegedly murdered and his assailant never brought to justice.

One landlord invited a psychic into the pub in order to assess the eerie goings-on, only to discover one of the rooms had a tragic past. The psychic refused to enter the room on the top floor, claiming a baby had died there in the 1800s under terrible circumstances. Many years later, a researcher was touring the pub and noticed something tucked behind the water tank up in the attic, directly above the room the psychic had refused to enter. She uncovered a sack containing old Victorian baby clothes, which disturbingly looked to have been cut with a knife.

The ghost of Ripper victim Annie Chapman is also thought to haunt the Ten Bells and to add to the chilling portfolio, reports of footsteps, disembodied laughter and claims of being shoved on the stairs by an invisible hand have also been heard over the years.

CELL BLOCK BOO

Ottawa Jail in Ottawa, Canada, was built in 1862 and conditions were harsh – with window spaces open to the elements, inmates froze in the winter and sweltered in the summer. The jail closed in 1972 and soon after it was converted into a youth hostel – but possibly the creepiest youth hostel around – which is still functioning today. Many original features have been kept, allowing guests to spend the night in a jail cell.

Visitors can take things several steps further and opt to catch some shut-eye in solitary confinement, tour death row, visit the unmarked graves of forgotten prisoners and peruse the original gallows.

Reports from guests offer an insight into an experience they'll never forget. Many overnighters have awoken to a shadowy figure standing at the foot of their bed, often reading a bible. Other guests have said they've seen a notorious hanged murderer in his old cell or wandering the hall on death row. One woman woke up with her arm in a phantom grip and other people say they were hummed to all night – which was apparently "an amazing experience" according to one guest.

Before the days of the youth hostel, a corner of the courtyard was dug up in the 1950s to make way for bridge foundations and 140 bodies of executed prisoners were discovered. One can

only imagine how many more lie under the rest of the concrete
– and where their spirits roam or might roam in the future…

ATACAMA GHOST TOWN

Deep in the expansive Atacama Desert, in northern Chile, lies a desolate ghost town, its ruined buildings crumbling in the intense heat of the scorching sun. La Noria was founded in 1826 as a saltpetre mining town and became home to thousands of residents, complete with shops, a school, church and railway station.

Historians believe many of those residing in La Noria were treated like slaves. Living and working conditions were harsh, with whole families expected to knuckle down and labour in the mines – many were worked to death in the intense heat. At the turn of the twentieth century, the town fell on hard times when a fire broke out, reducing its saltpetre deposits, and by the time of the First World War a synthetic alternative had been discovered.

With nothing left for them there, the residents left and La Noria was eventually abandoned. Many structures remained and former residents' possessions could be found in abundance. The town suffered at the hands of many looters, sifting through the left-behind belongings and even digging up the graves of the dead to rob valuables from the coffins that lay within.

Today, many coffins in the graveyard are exposed, showing the bodies that had been interred, and bones are scattered all around. A visit to La Noria is not for the faint-hearted – not only is the scene both sad and grisly, many deep mine shafts remain, causing severe danger underfoot. Add to that the fact that, thanks to the disturbance of the resting dead in the graveyard, this place is considered to be extremely haunted and you'd be forgiven for thinking you might give it a miss.

Nonetheless, fearless daytime visitors have reported hearing footsteps, voices and even screams when there is clearly no one around. Others claim to have witnessed the dead rising after sunset, making their way out of the graveyard and into the town, where they wander the ruins, angry and confused by the upset of what was supposed to have been their final resting place.

GRUESOME GREEN LADY

Château de Brissac in the Loire Valley in western France has an extensive history. Built in the eleventh century and rebuilt in the sixteenth, many have passed through its doors and called it home. And, you guessed it, many a tragedy has occurred.

One of these tragedies involved a woman who was brutally murdered by her husband in the grounds of the château in the fifteenth century. Many have spied her ghostly presence in the tower room of the chapel and as she is always wearing a green dress she has become aptly known as the Green Lady.

The current Duke of Brissac and his family have got rather used to her wandering from room to room, and mortal and phantom exist side by side. When guests encounter the Green Lady, however, they are generally terrified. Should you glimpse her face you would see black, gaping holes where her eyes and nose should be, as if looking at the face of a corpse.

ETERNAL LIGHTHOUSE RESIDENTS

The lighthouse in St Augustine, Florida, is thought to be so haunted that paranormal investigators and camera crews have made more than a few trips up its curving staircase, and a scout around on the internet will reveal footage of what they discovered.

Built in 1874, the man charged with overseeing construction of the lighthouse brought his family to St Augustine to live close to the site. His three daughters used to play on the construction site, riding in the old railway cart used by the builders down to the water. The builders set up a wooden board to ensure the cart would stop before it reached the water. However, one day, unbeknown to the girls, the board wasn't there and the cart continued all the way into the water, flipped over and trapped the girls in the sea. The elder two daughters drowned in this heart-breaking accident and construction shut down, along with the rest of the town, as a mark of respect for the girls. The family returned to their hometown of Maine to put them to rest.

There have been numerous reports over the years from lighthouse keepers, their families and visitors, of a paranormal presence at the St Augustine lighthouse. One recalls waking up in the neighbouring keeper's house one night to find a small girl standing next to his bed but upon blinking a few times she had disappeared. Those who claim to have encountered the spirits of the children say they are playful, with one visitor recalling how her shoelace was tied to the staircase and a staff member finding himself in the middle of a ghostly game of hide and seek. Upon closing up for the night, he heard giggling at the top of the tower and so went to investigate, but there was no one there. He then descended the tower, only to hear the giggling once again, but from below.

Another hide-and-seek story saw a group of young women visit the basement of the keeper's home on a tour, bringing with them an EMF meter, designed to measure the electrical activity in the room. One woman held the meter and asked the girls if they would like to play hide and seek. The meter spiked and she went looking around the basement using the EMF meter to locate them. Finding EMF activity when she searched under the stairs, she deduced she had located the girls and asked if they would like to play once more. Again, the meter spiked and she searched for them until there was further activity on the meter and she believed she had found them. However, when other visitors entered the room the meter went silent.

The children have been oft sighted too, with one woman on a tour complimenting a fellow guest on her daughter's good behaviour. She was confused, she didn't have a daughter and there were no children on the tour that evening, but the woman insisted she had seen a little girl at her side throughout the visit. Multiple sightings of girls in Victorian dress have been reported over the years in and around the lighthouse, making it one of the most haunted spots in North America.

ABANDON ALL HOPE

The Castle of Good Hope sits in Cape Town, South Africa, inland from its original location on Table Bay. First built in the seventeenth century, the fortress was declared a national monument in the 1930s and is widely considered to be the best surviving example of a Dutch East India Company fort.

The castle has been inhabited by many a phantom over the years, with reports of eerie occurrences plentiful. A woman dressed in grey has been spotted running through the castle, crying hysterically with her hands to her face. During more recent excavations a woman's body was unearthed and given a proper burial – the woman in grey hasn't been seen since this happened.

In the 1700s a soldier was found hanging from the bell rope in the castle's bell tower. The tower was sealed off after his death, however to this day the bell has been heard to occasionally ring on its own.

Another reported haunting is that of a tall man seen jumping off one of the castle walls. He is thought to be a former occupant who sentenced a group of soldiers to death and was cursed by one of them shortly before the execution. He was found later that night, slumped over his desk, dead, with a look of pure terror on his face, and some believe he is forced to haunt the castle grounds forever.

PERIL IN PERU

In the heart of downtown Lima lies a house that locals say is so haunted it can make you lose your mind. La Casa Matusita was built in the 1700s and legend has it that the house's very first occupant had something to do with the events that took place hundreds of years later.

This first resident was accused of witchcraft and sorcery, for which she was eventually burned at the stake. The story goes that she placed a curse on the house from the middle of the bonfire as it engulfed her.

Many years later a cruel man lived in the house who treated his servants very badly. One day they took revenge. When their boss was hosting a dinner party, the servants added powerful hallucinogens to the food and drink and then hid in the kitchen to wait for them to take effect. To their horror, upon returning to the dining room some time later, they found an incredibly gruesome scene. Bodies were strewn around the room, decapitated and mutilated, the walls splattered with blood. The servants are said to have spent the rest of their lives in the city asylum.

A century after the dinner party bloodbath, another tragedy occurred under the roof of La Casa Matusita. A Japanese family – the Matusitas, from where the house gets its name –

lived happily within its walls, but it wasn't long before many believe the dark spirits of the house took hold. The father of the family developed anger issues and violent tendencies, and upon returning from work one day to find his wife in bed with another man he took a knife from the kitchen and stabbed her. He didn't stop there. He also killed their children and then himself.

In the 1970s, a famous South American TV personality declared he could spend seven days and nights at the house to prove it was not haunted as people claimed it to be. After just four hours, he emerged from La Casa Matusita babbling and terrified. Later in life he spent some years in a psychiatric facility and refused to ever speak of his experiences in the house that day, as long as he lived.

BUMP IN THE NIGHT AT THE BOLIVAR

Not far from La Casa Matusita sits a seriously haunted hotel. Lima's Gran Hotel Bolivar is considered one of the spookiest buildings in Peru. Built in 1924, this is the kind of place that has entertained high-ranking politicians, writers and celebrities over the years, its striking interiors of stained glass and marble floors capturing the era of its inception. The Rolling Stones were thrown out of the hotel for debauched behaviour, while literary royalty Ernest Hemingway and William Faulkner have propped up the bar, and Charles de Gaulle, Richard Nixon and Robert Kennedy attempted some shut-eye within the bedrooms.

The Bolivar's glamour has faded in more recent years and according to eyewitnesses spectral residents have moved in. The hallways are often wandered by figures from the past, with guests claiming to have come across a woman in white roaming up and down before simply disappearing. There has also been talk of another ghostly apparition, of a suicide victim who allegedly threw herself from one of the windows at the top of the hotel and fell to the street below. She reputedly searches the corridors of the hotel for a way to cross over into the afterlife.

Former employees are also thought to haunt the hotel floors, with a ghostly bellboy appearing and disappearing in various parts of the hotel, and a former security guard has been seen carrying out his duties on the upper floors of the hotel long after his death.

The creepiest parts of the hotel are rumoured to be at the top, on floors five and six, which have been sealed off to both guests and staff members, left for many years to gather dust. The hotel owners claim the floors are off limits for financial reasons, but many believe that blisteringly high levels of paranormal activity are the real reason for the closure.

HITCHHIKER HEADS FOR HOME

In Port Wakefield, South Australia, there have been recurrent sightings of a ghostly hitchhiker since the 1940s. On a long and lonely stretch of road when making the drive from Adelaide to the Yorke Peninsula, many a traveller has reported picking up or interacting with a hitchhiker who has then disappeared without trace.

On a particularly stormy and dark evening, one young couple recounted stopping to pick up a man dressed in what appeared to be an air force uniform, attempting to hitch a lift by the side of the road. He asked if they would take him to an address in Adelaide and he sat in the back seat of their car. Upon arrival at the house however, the couple turned to find he was no longer sitting in the car and had seemingly vanished into thin air.

Utterly bewildered, the couple knocked on the door of the house to see if the occupants could shed any light on their bizarre experience. A woman answered the door and told the couple her son had died in a plane crash during air force training in the Second World War. The flight had taken off in nearby Mallala and although her son's body had been recovered it was buried in an unknown location. She believed his spirit was trying to "come home".

TERROR AT THE TOWER

Possibly the most haunted landmark in the city, the Tower of London looms menacingly over the Thames, a reminder of a bloody and unforgiving history of torture and execution. Built in 1078 by William the Conqueror, the tower has been a royal residence, the home of the Crown Jewels, an armoury, treasury and public record office, but perhaps most famously it was used as a prison and place of torture – with executions taking place either within the grounds or on nearby Tower Hill.

Perhaps the most famous of the tower's ghosts is Anne Boleyn, Henry VIII's second wife, who was beheaded at the tower for alleged adultery. Her headless apparition has been sighted wandering the halls of the tower close to the scene of her death.

Lady Jane Grey – great-niece of Henry VIII who was ill-advised to make a bid for the throne following the death of Henry's son Edward VI and was executed at the age of 17 after her nine-day reign – was noticed by a guardsman in the 1950s. Lady Jane's husband, Lord Guildford Dudley, who was also executed for his part in her brief reign, is thought to haunt his former cell in the Beauchamp Tower and his ghost is allegedly responsible for the word "Jane" carved into the wall.

Henry VI, who was murdered while praying in the Wakefield Tower, is said to haunt the spot where he died, appearing every year on the anniversary of his death as the clock strikes midnight. While Sir Walter Raleigh, imprisoned twice at the tower and eventually put to death there, is said to wander along the battlements known as "Raleigh's Walk" and his presence has been reported in the Bloody Tower where he was held.

The so-called Princes in the Tower, the deposed Edward V and Richard Duke of York, were the only sons of Edward IV, declared illegitimate and locked up in the tower in the 1480s. After the princes went missing it was assumed they had been murdered and two sets of children's bones later discovered beneath a staircase were widely accepted to be theirs. Although this remains disputed to this day. The sad, creepy sight of two little boys, dressed in white nightshirts and holding hands, has often been reported in the White Tower. Many have also seen them playing on the battlements and have even heard the sound of children giggling.

LONELY IN THE CITY

In Ho Chi Minh City in Vietnam, a mysterious presence haunts the museum of art. Rumour has it the ghost of a young girl strolls the corridors moaning and professing her loneliness. When it was built in 1934, the building that now houses the museum was first used as offices for a successful business, headed up by an extremely wealthy real estate magnate who owned around 20,000 properties across the city. The building later became the magnate's sprawling family home.

The property tycoon's daughter contracted leprosy and was confined to her bedroom on the top floor of the building. The family considered the disease to be a curse and hid her illness from everyone outside the household. Eventually the family announced she had died from a different illness and even held a funeral.

The girl was kept locked in her room, her meals passed to her through a slot in the door. She grew more and more lonely and miserable before taking her own life.

Since her death and the eventual conversion of the building into a museum, there have been multiple sightings of an ethereal figure of a girl in the halls and reports of disembodied crying at night.

ANCIENT REVENGE

In Chinese legend there exists the story of the ghost of Tu-Po. He served as a minister to the Emperor Husan (827–783 BC), but the two had a disagreement and Husan ordered the death of Tu-Po. Husan had been warned that if he did this he would have a serious haunting on his hands – Tu-Po would come back and seek revenge for the slaying. Despite this, the emperor didn't listen and went ahead with the horrific murder anyway.

It turns out Tu-Po was up for more than a bit of mild haunting. A stunned assembly of feudal lords looked on as a ghostly apparition of former minister Tu-Po fired an arrow at the emperor, killing him on the spot.

ATHENS IN CHAINS

Pliny the Younger, a Roman lawyer and writer born in AD 61, told a story supposedly rooted in Greek legend that is sufficiently supernatural to have survived the test of time.

He alleged that in Athens there stood a house with a reputation for being a little too far on the spooky side. People were too scared to live there, so it lay uninhabited. At one point the house had been lived in, but at night, people could hear the sound of chains rattling and iron clashing and clanking, and many saw a ghostly apparition of an emaciated old man with a long beard rattling the chains securing his limbs.

The house was abandoned and a brave philosopher moved in. He had a plan to wait for the ghost and attempt to converse with it. Sure enough, in the dead of night, the phantasmal man appeared and did his chain-rattling around the philosopher, before vanishing.

The philosopher marked the spot where the man had disappeared and arranged for the floor to be dug up. So the story goes, a decomposing body of a man in chains was found beneath the floor. A proper burial was arranged and the ghost was never seen again.

DEMONS
AND SPIRITS

In all cultures there lurk hundreds of demons, rooted firmly in folklore, but in some cases woven into the fabric of society. For thousands of years, demons have pervaded religion, instilling fear in worshippers. Many even believe that demons can cross into our world and take control of us, communicating through humans who must then be exorcized.

It is, however, important to remember that throughout history some of these cases will have been misdiagnosed, and with modern advancements in medical knowledge surrounding mental health and psychosis, perhaps some of them would have been dealt with differently.

Bear in mind the ubiquity of superstition in the past, when many believed that demons could possess dolls and animals, and even lurk in the bathroom waiting for you to knock. And then there are the children walking backward up the wall – you heard me right. Read on.

Let's not forget the more benign spirits – sometimes that poltergeist is merely projecting, often literally, its tantrums; toddler-like and attention-seeking as it tries to get its resident human to take notice of its needs. At other times, of course, the poltergeist just wants you out of their house and the physical and violent nature of the haunting can be terrifying and ultimately life-wrecking.

Read the stories for yourself and test your beliefs – how would you deal with these powerful paranormal episodes?

BROUHAHA IN BATTERSEA

"Poltergeist" is a German word meaning "noisy ghost". Folklorists describe them as attention-seeking, like the toddler of the spirit world – tantruming when people don't take notice of it. This description certainly matches up with the behaviour displayed by these powerful and at times chilling spirits. Poltergeists have been known to turn people's lives upside down, drive them from their homes and cause serious injury. The harassment usually comes in stages, starting with noises, before building up to objects moving and spirit-vandalism in the form of messages scrawled on the walls and violent chaos.

The case of the Battersea poltergeist saw a family living in a small unassuming terraced house in 1950s suburban London subjected to years of nightmarish behaviour from their uninvited house guest. The Hitchings family first encountered their "guest" in 1956 when daughter Shirley found an ornate silver key on her pillow. No one recognized it and it didn't fit any locks in the house. That night there was a sound of deafening banging, so loud and harsh were the thuds that they shook the walls and floors of the house. The Second World War had ended less than a decade before and the Hitchings had lived through the Blitz, likening their ghostly experience to that of living through war.

DEMONS AND SPIRITS

Neighbours banged on the door to complain, thinking the family were pulling up floorboards or hammering on the walls in the middle of the night. The police were called and heard the noises from the street. The banging continued and became a nightly event. The family called in tradespeople, hoping they might be able to explain why the house was making so much noise. No one could. The noises kept coming, and in the daytime too. The family began to hear scratching that sounded as if it was coming from within the furniture itself and particularly inside the headboard of the bed, preventing them from sleep. Needless to say, it wasn't long before they were all incredibly sleep deprived. There were plenty of witnesses beyond the family to back up this strange and eerie phenomenon.

Following the advice of an investigator, the family came to terms with the fact they were dealing with a poltergeist and realized the presence had a particular preoccupation with their 15-year-old daughter Shirley, who experienced more of the spirit's attention than anyone else.

Soon the family were hearing noises of objects seemingly being thrown around – with reports of a clock floating through the air, sheets flying off beds, pots and pans being launched from an empty room and slippers walking around on their own. It wasn't long before the behaviour escalated to involve the spirit attempting to communicate with the family. Messages were scrawled on walls and bits of paper. The poltergeist, whom the family named "Donald", would pen notes to Shirley saying things like "Shirley I come" in chilling scrawled writing. The media picked up the story and decided Donald had a sinister obsession with the teenager, discovering he would even leave the house and follow her to work.

The ordeal lasted for 12 years, during which time the family stayed put and various mediums came and went, the investigator often camping out in the house to record the activity. The case even made the news and was mentioned in the House of Commons. The stress of housing Donald forced Shirley's father to give up work, but when the poltergeist finally left the house – by scrawling the word "goodbye" on a piece of paper and taking the key that had appeared on the first night – Shirley's mother went into mourning. Over the course of more than a decade, the family had grown to know Donald and even discovered things about his life before the haunting.

Shirley is still alive and has been interviewed about her experience many times, most recently for the BBC podcast *The Battersea Poltergeist*, a mix of drama and documentary. Several books have been written on the topic too, the case thrilling and intriguing so many, with *The Poltergeist Prince of London* written by Shirley herself.

TIE A YELLOW RIBBON

In the culture of Myanmar, formerly Burma, in Southeast Asia, is the story of the Ma Phae War, which translates as "yellow ribbon lady". Considered the guardian spirit of burial grounds, she is a *nat* – a spirit of which there are many types in Burmese folklore.

This *nat* is also a harbinger of death. She supposedly leaves the graveyard at midnight, carrying a coffin on her shoulder and wanders through town – shuffling unnervingly, her long hair flowing behind her – before placing the coffin on the doorstep of one of the houses. Apparently, a member of that family – usually a child – will sicken and die soon afterwards.

As recently as the 1990's a highly respected Buddhist monk said he had been visited by the Ma Phae War in a dream. He alleged she told him she wanted to eat the flesh of babies and that he attempted to persuade her to eat the flesh of nearby dogs instead. Parents were so frightened at the thought that they put up signs outside their houses at night that read "Our baby's flesh is bitter but our dog's flesh is sweet".

EXORCISM OF ROLAND DOE

In 1949, in a small town in Maryland, USA, a 14-year-old boy was exorcized multiple times for displaying demonic behaviour.

The case was well known, but the boy's identity was kept secret until much later on and instead he was referred to as "Roland Doe". (His real name we now know was Ronald Hunkeler.) He was an only child, relying on his adult family members to play with him. He took a great interest in the Ouija board his aunt introduced him to, and it was through use of this that he allegedly became possessed.

Following the death of his aunt, the family began to experience a presence in the house. Strange noises, banging and tapping, as well as household objects levitating all became a regular occurrence. Roland's parents observed that this activity only happened when he was nearby and the boy's mattress had even been known to float up into the air with him on it.

They turned to the church for help and Roland was put under overnight observation at the home of a pastor, away from the family house. Sure enough, items started moving around the room, furniture scraped along the floor and a vase floated through the air. The family were advised to call in Catholic priests. Roland was subjected to a number of exorcisms to rid his body of what the priests believed was a demon residing in it.

DEMONS AND SPIRITS

A large group of clergymen attended one of the exorcisms and eyewitness accounts detailed Roland manipulating objects and causing them to fly through the air, his bed shaking violently and him speaking in an infernal, guttural voice that shocked and appalled all present. He displayed a severe aversion to anything religious, recoiling from crucifixes, bibles and holy words, and on one occasion squeezed a hand out of one of his restraints to remove a bedspring from beneath him and attacked a priest with the sharp end of it.

Roland was eventually admitted to a psychiatric hospital where further exorcisms were performed. Priests claimed the words "hell" and "evil" appeared across the flesh of Roland's body and he lashed out violently.

The demon was eventually successfully exorcized and, whatever the truth of that, Roland went on to live a normal life. At least one of the priests involved ended up needing extensive treatment in a psychiatric hospital.

The case of Roland Doe was the inspiration for William Peter Blatty's chilling 1971 novel *The Exorcist*, which in 1973 was transformed into the film of the same name that well and truly shocked the world – and, it's fair to say, damaged the reputation of the Ouija board and heavily dampened its once roaring trade.

STAY OUT OF THE WATER

In Japanese fable you will find a curious little amphibious demon known as the Kappa. Translating as "river child", the Kappa is of a similar size to a human child, usually green and humanoid, but with webbed hands and feet and the shell of a turtle on its back.

An interesting trait is the cavity on its head, filled with water and regarded as the source of the creature's power. Should this water be spilled or dried up, the Kappa will be severely weakened and could even die.

Now, the Kappa is curious for several reasons. It is known as a troublemaker and a pest, but can also be friendly. Its behaviour can be as wild as it can be mild, one moment befriending humans and animals, and doing them multiple favours, and the next attacking viciously, drowning people and animals, kidnapping children, raping women and eating its victims – usually their flesh or liver and sometimes even drinking their blood. Horses and cows are particularly vulnerable to the Kappa and even today signs next to bodies of water in Japan warn against the dangers of the creature.

It also has a penchant for sumo wrestling and cucumbers – and offerings of the vegetable are frequently made during Japanese festivals. In times gone by people would often write the names of family members on cucumbers and send them down the river as peace offerings to the Kappa.

In order to defeat a Kappa, one must cause it to spill the liquid from the cavity on its head, without which it will die. It will retreat if confronted with ginger, sesame or items made from iron. Its arms can also be easily pulled off and doing so causes it to relent in the hope you will return its limbs, which can be reattached.

Interestingly, a type of *hosomaki* sushi filled with cucumber is named after the creature, so remember that next time you order your *kappamaki*.

BEWARE THE SLENDER MAN

This demon story from modern times is interesting because it was manufactured and its creator never denied that, but it went on to influence the actions of a handful of teenagers who claim it inspired in them violent, life-threatening behaviour.

In 2009, an American graphic designer responded to a competition online in which the entrants were asked to create paranormal images along the theme of modern myth using existing photographs as their jumping-off point.

He took two photographs from the 1980s of children playing and added a sinister figure in the background. This figure was very tall and thin, towering over the children. He was dressed in a black suit, with dark and skinny tentacle-like protrusions and no facial features, his face human but blank. He wrote underneath the pictures that the young people in the photographs as well as the photographer had gone missing.

The creepy photographs and story behind them were convincing enough that they went viral and more images of Slender Man started cropping up around the internet. Some images were from modern times while others showed Slender Man in photographs from bygone eras – what they all had in common was the black suit, the extraordinary height, the rake-like physique and the featureless face.

The internet lost its mind – people started creating masses of Slender Man images, countless stories were being written about him and fan art appeared all over the place. Slender Man had entered the world of urban legend – a super-macabre betentacled skinny giant bogeyman who would creep out of the woods and abduct children.

The tale took a turn when in 2014 in Wisconsin, USA, two 14-year-old girls were accused of stabbing their classmate 19 times, claiming they had done so in order to appease Slender Man and keep him from hurting them or their families. Their victim survived, but only just. They had first come across Slender Man online when they were 12 and become obsessed with him.

Other crimes related to the case include a 13-year-old in Ohio attacking her mother with a knife, all in the name of Slender Man, and a few months later a 14-year-old in Florida set her house on fire after being exposed to the scary figure.

In 2019 a documentary was released telling the Slender Man story and how it plagued the imaginations of country's youth and inspired a handful of them to do some seriously awful things. The powers of even an entirely fabricated demon in this instance were truly disturbing.

FOLD YOUR LAUNDRY

Pontianak, the capital of the province of West Kalimantan in Indonesia, was built on the territory of a malevolent spirit after which it is named.

In Southeast Asian legend, the Pontianak is a vicious female spirit that lives in rivers and swamps – usually at a crossing point – and takes the form of a beautiful woman to prey on men, children and the vulnerable. In some versions, she can shape-shift into a vampiric creature and feed on mortals, eating their liver and drinking their blood.

In the late 1700s, despite warnings he was on Pontianak territory, a man decided to set up a trading post at the crossing point of the Kapuas and Landak rivers. It is reputed that the spirit creature soon emerged to prey on the man and his workers, so they fought back. They fired cannon into the swamp in an attempt to destroy the nest of the Pontianak and leave the area clear for their new trading post. It seemed to work.

The scent of fresh, drying laundry will purportedly attract a Pontianak and for this reason many Malaysians are superstitious about leaving clothes out drying overnight.

POLTERGEIST IN LONG ISLAND

Often claimed to be the true story behind the Steven Spielberg-penned horror movie sensation *Poltergeist* (1982), in 1958 a terrifying presence terrorized a whole family in an intense series of disturbances over the course of five weeks.

The Herrmann family lived in Long Island, New York, in the small town of Seaford. One evening, the mother was at home with her two children when they heard popping noises from all around the house. They went to investigate, only to find uncapped bottles of various things – from cosmetics to cleaning products, and even a vial of holy water that had been spilled everywhere.

She called her husband, who was still at work, but he dismissed her fears, and said it was likely a prank perpetrated by kids in the neighbourhood. However, the following night the same thing happened again. It also happened the night after that and then the strange presence started moving bottles around in front of the family, so they called the police.

The police turned up to a scene of bottle tops popping off left, right and centre and performed several tests to check for electrical disturbances but they found no evidence of any.

Once the Herrmanns realized there was no logical explanation for what they were experiencing, they called in a priest. Experts suggested they were dealing with a poltergeist but everyone was baffled as to why one would be residing in their new-build house. The Herrmanns were the only people to have lived there, which didn't fit the usual poltergeist theory of ex-resident spirits with unfinished business. It was also suggested that the presence of adolescents might be what was attracting the spirit to the house – a supposed draw for poltergeists – and enhancing its mischievous behaviour.

The Herrmanns' subjection to the paranormal activity didn't last long – although it was severe, with 70 reported counts of poltergeist behaviour – five weeks later it stopped and the family assumed the spirit had left. They moved out of the house and moved on with their lives.

Poltergeist the movie was more far-fetched than the experience of the Herrmanns, with portals, skeletons and ancient burial grounds all thrown into the mix, but their story is at its root – just given the Hollywood treatment.

PRETA MANGER

In Thai folklore there is a spirit doomed to suffer for all eternity. The supposedly once wicked humans, the Preta paid penance by being reborn as these sad and tortured creatures of the night.

Preta translates as "hungry ghost", the creature being punished with a seemingly insatiable appetite – so much so that they sometimes resort to eating their own flesh.

They are invisible to humans, but there is a belief they can be seen or felt by some people when in a certain mental state. The Preta are thought to be vaguely human-like, bony, with mummified skin, scrawny limbs and a long neck. They have a bulging, hungry belly and their mouths are tiny, their throats incredibly narrow, to add to their anguish and punishment in the afterlife. They are allegedly often seen licking up pools of water in temples, desperate to sate their thirst.

It seems they are made to suffer at all times and in all temperatures – the moon supposedly burning them in summer and the sun freezing them in the winter.

They do not harm humans and are considered no more than a nuisance, their main purpose on Earth to suffer for the crimes of their past life.

CONJURING SPIRITS

In the small town of Harrisville, Rhode Island, USA, sits an eighteenth-century farmhouse with a history of some serious paranormal activity. As with all the best horror stories, this one is set in a peaceful, beautiful plot of land on the edge of the suburbs. Quiet, quaint, but wait...

During the 1970s, Carolyn Perron, along with her husband and five daughters, moved into the house. Almost immediately they felt a presence and began to experience unusual activity. The broom would move to a different place from where it had been left, or sometimes disappear altogether, and piles of dirt or rubbish would appear in the middle of a freshly swept floor. These occurrences were pretty harmless, the family thought, but things were about to get worse.

The whole family would wake up at 5.15 a.m., their beds shaking, and a foul stench of something akin to rotting flesh would engulf certain areas of the house. Events moved up a notch when objects started flying across the room and smashed into the wall on the other side. Glass shattered, doors slammed and one evening Carolyn was sitting quietly when she felt a piercing pain in her leg only to discover she had been injured – a puncture wound on her leg began oozing blood, as if she had been stabbed with a large needle, but none was to be found.

The Perrons realized they were sharing their home with a poltergeist and decided to research the history of the house. A woman called Bathsheba Sherman had lived there in the mid-1800s and as far as the Perrons could tell she considered herself the mistress of the house even from the depths of the afterlife and had it in for Carolyn. Local rumour suggested Bathsheba had practised witchcraft and taken part in satanic rituals, for the purpose of which she allegedly killed an infant with a large sewing needle to the brain, although she was never convicted of that crime.

The Perrons invited well-respected paranormal investigators to examine the house and encounter the spirit of Bathsheba for themselves. Upon holding a seance, Carolyn became possessed and began speaking in tongues. Those present said her chair rose into the air and her daughter – who had not been allowed in but was watching through a crack in the door – later said she thought she was going to pass out when she witnessed this.

The family were plagued by the spirits for several more years, staying in the house until 1980 and moving as soon as they could afford to. Once they left, however, they said the spirits never bothered them again.

The house was bought by two paranormal investigators in 2019, who claim to have witnessed doors opening on their own, and heard disembodied voices, footsteps and knocking. They plan to tastefully renovate the house and, equally as tastefully, open it up for paranormal tours.

The Perrons' house provided the inspiration for hit horror flick *The Conjuring*, from James Wan who directed *Saw* and *Insidious*, other equally terrifying feature-length nightmares.

TERRIFYING TOILET SPIRIT

In Japanese schools there's a myth about a spirit girl who lives in the bathroom. Hanako-san hangs around in school bathrooms, waiting for children to enter so she has a playmate.

Depending from which part of Japan you hear the story, she might have been a child who was killed in the school bathroom during a game of hide and seek, when a bomb fell on the school in the Second World War; or she might be have been murdered in the toilet and her spirit lives on.

She usually occupies the bathroom on the third floor of a school and can be summoned by knocking three times on the door of the third stall and asking for Hanako-san. If she is there, she will reply. Some stories state a ghostly or bloody hand will appear and pull the visitor into the stall.

What happens next could be very sweet or completely terrifying. Hanako-san may simply be lonely and want to play with you, or she may want to drag you into the toilet itself and straight through a portal into hell. Some stories even suggest she may transform into a giant lizard – with three heads in one version – and devour you right there for invading her privacy.

Knocking on that third door seems like a bit of a gamble now, doesn't it?

DON'T FALL ASLEEP

It's not uncommon to suffer from sleep paralysis – finding yourself suspended in between the worlds of slumber and consciousness but unable to physically move your body. There are, of course, reasonable explanations as to why this happens, but in tales spanning different cultures across the globe certain night creatures can be responsible.

In Brazil, La Pisadeira is a tall and thin woman with red eyes and long yellow fingernails. She stalks along rooftops and enters people's houses, hiding and watching as they eat a big family meal. She will wait until they retire to bed on a full stomach and drift off to sleep. Then she will sit on one of their chests so they cannot move. Her victim will open their eyes, in a bleary-eyed, semi-dream state and find themselves unable to move.

People have reported experiencing sleep paralysis and the feeling that a malevolent spirit was present, hovering over them as they lie helplessly in bed.

European versions of La Pisadeira speak of an "old hag" who similarly causes sleep paralysis by sitting on her prey and suffocating them. She is also alleged to "swallow" the voices of her victims as they cry out in a state of semi-consciousness mid-smothering. The following morning, the unfortunate will often complain of ill health or exhaustion and, as legend would have it, on the morning after the third or fourth attack by the old hag the victim would be dead.

"Don't fall asleep" doesn't sound like such terrible advice after all, does it?

DEVIL AT PLAY

In the 1630s in Loudun, France, parish priest Urbain Grandier was accused of making a pact with the Devil and in turn being responsible for the demonic possession of a group of nuns.

The nuns claimed to have been visited by the Devil; they also said Grandier had sexually assaulted them. Their possession saw them barking, screaming obscenities and contorting themselves violently. They also reported having visions of the dead.

Many public exorcisms were performed and, as word got around, people liked to come and watch as priests attempted to rid the nuns of the Devil, and the unusual behaviour associated with it.

During Grandier's trial, a document was produced as evidence that appeared to be the pact he had signed with the Devil and various other demons. The parchment was signed by Grandier, as well as Satan, Leviathan, Astaroth and other demonic beings.

In 1634 Grandier was found guilty of witchcraft and burned at the stake.

EXORCISM SCHOOL

Every year, the Vatican throws open its doors and welcomes priests from all over the world to take part in its annual exorcism course.

As many as 250 priests from 50 different countries flock to Rome in order to brush up on or learn from scratch how to spot a demonic possession.

Priests will attend a series of lectures looking at past exorcisms, led by priests who have performed them. The topics of these talks include identification of a demonic presence in a human and the rituals involved in expelling them from the body.

The course, entitled "Exorcism and the Prayer of Liberation", has been running since 2005 and is the only one of its kind, which is why so many priests make the long journey to take part. It covers the theological, anthropological and psychological background to exorcisms.

In Italy alone, 500,000 people a year reportedly request exorcisms and the Pope has told priests to send members of their congregation to an exorcist if they believe there is a "genuine spiritual disturbance" at play.

FACE TO FACE WITH THE DEVIL

A serial exorcist priest from Rome claimed that one occasion when he was called to the aid of a young man chilled him to the bone. Despite claiming to have conducted some 60,000 exorcisms in his 30-year-long demon-banishing career, the priest experienced something that day that he would never forget.

When a man was brought to him showing signs of demonic possession, the priest immediately felt an overwhelming presence of evil. The priest called out to Jesus, asking him to help to cleanse his patient. The man began to spit and curse in English, instead of Italian (his mother tongue). He directed his words at the priest and attempted to physically attack him.

The priest claimed that the demon "burst forth and looked straight at him, drooling saliva from the young man's mouth". He shouted prayers at the demon, as he had done during possessions for so many years, but this was different.

The priest bellowed, "Unclean spirit! Whoever you are and all your companions who possess this servant of God, I command you: tell me your name."

The man stared at him, snarled, and said with bitter and sinister tones, "I am Lucifer."

The priest was horrified at this admission, but he kept going – he knew he must rid this poor man of the demon that resided within him. And – apparently – that's just what he did.

The priest opened up about his life spent exorcizing, explaining how patients would be treated in a tiny room tucked away from the streets and people, so they would not be able to hear the screams. He claimed he always carried two wooden crucifixes, holy water and consecrated oil – essential exorcism tools – and that the possessed usually needed several exorcisms in order to get the job done, with patients cured in a matter of months or in some cases not for several years.

CLIMBING THE WALLS

In 2014, in Indianapolis, Indiana, USA, a family claimed to have been possessed by demons. A mother and her three children moved into a property on a quiet street only to find that one cold December day their enclosed porch was engulfed with a swarm of huge black flies. They killed the flies, but they kept coming back. At midnight each night they would hear the sound of heavy boots on the basement steps and the door creak open, but there was never anyone there. They locked the door, but the noises continued. They also saw shadowy figures in the living room.

One night the 12-year-old allegedly levitated above her bed – the family and house guests surrounded her and began praying. When the child finally descended, she awoke with no memory of what had happened.

The family called on the churches in the area but most didn't want to know. One church was kind and told them to bleach the house and draw crosses on every door and window using oil. The family also reached out to several mediums – one of whom visited the house and claimed it was besieged by at least 200 demons. They told the family they should move house, but they couldn't afford to.

They burned sage and sulphur around the house, constructed an altar in the basement and read passages from the bible on the advice of the medium. They had three days of respite from the unusual occurrences but after that, things took a turn for the worse.

The mother claimed her children all became possessed – she described how their eyes would bulge, wicked smiles would cross their faces and their voices became deep and guttural. The grandmother, who also lived in the house, claimed she escaped possession because she had a guardian spirit protecting her. However, her daughter, the children's mother, also fell foul of demonic possession and would be prone to fits of shaking and overheating.

The children described seeing and talking to spirit children. They were thrown across rooms by paranormal forces and the 12-year-old spoke of being held down and choked by invisible hands. The family were often forced to take refuge in a nearby motel.

Medical staff attending the house watched in horror as one of the children was lifted into the air by invisible forces and flung against a wall. Later on, at the police station, more witnesses saw the same child walk up the wall and perform a backflip back down to the floor.

The family finally found a priest willing to assist them. He visited the house and after spending many hours examining the different rooms confirmed the presence of demons; he also claimed the house was haunted by ghosts. After multiple exorcisms of the family members and the house, the home seemed to have been banished of evil spirits – they went quiet, and the family didn't report being bothered by them again.

THE ROSENHEIM POLTERGEIST

In 1967 in Rosenheim, Germany, a parapsychologist was called upon to investigate some strange goings-on at an office, disturbances that were only occurring at the weekends.

Maintenance staff alleged that lighting fixtures were exploding, swinging back and forth or their bulbs being mysteriously removed. A heavy filing cabinet supposedly moved across the office of its own accord, along with other bulky furniture. Remarkably, a framed painting on the wall was filmed spinning around and when these unusual happenings were reported to the company providing power to the office it produced evidence of strange electricity surges from the building.

Experts gave a verdict of poltergeist activity, claiming there must be a spirit force or energy at work, but the parapsychologist had different ideas. He claimed the electrical disturbances were caused by the emotions of a young secretary who worked in the office. He speculated that her unhappiness had been converted into psychokinesis and was causing the strange electrical interferences and objects to move around.

Apparently, the secretary was frustrated and unhappy with her work and depressed about her love life.

The parapsychologist felt vindicated when she moved away, left her job and the disturbances ceased.

HOUNDS OF HELL

In English folklore the black dog is a diabolical creature – not every black dog of course, there are plenty of non-evil ones. The black dog of demonology is an unusually large hound with red or yellow eyes that glow wildly. The black dog is thought of as an omen of death, and is said to often appear on ancient pathways, at places of execution, on crossroads and during electrical storms.

Depending on which part of England, the black dog of doom takes many different names – Barghest, Black Shuck, Padfoot (see what you did there, J. K. Rowling), Swooning Shadow, Bogey Beast, Shug Monkey or Hairy Jack, among others.

On Dartmoor in Devon, a huntsman was alleged to have sold his soul to the Devil and when he died black dogs surrounded his grave. His ghost is said to ride with black dogs and this fable inspired Arthur Conan Doyle's world-famous Sherlock Holmes novel *The Hound of the Baskervilles*.

The stories are manifold: some say the dog will chase anyone who crosses its path, others that a spectral black dog haunts the local countryside, bridges, castles or the town's streets. In one region the hound is headless, although it can be heard barking into the dark. The folkloric history of the black dog runs so deep that often local landmarks and hostelries are named in its honour.

In Jersey, a black dog appears to warn of an incoming storm; in Newgate, London, a black dog haunted the prison, appearing before executions. While in Guernsey the black dog appears to someone for whom death is imminent and in Cornwall the black dogs are hellhounds that hunt with the Devil and sometimes have human heads. Giving the legend a positive spin, in Somerset the black dog is a gentle and loving spirit that plays with children and appears to lost or lonely travellers, accompanying them on their way when they need a guide.

TARZAN OF THE UNDERWORLD

An Oni, found in Japanese narrative tradition, is a grotesque ogre-like demon. A hulking figure with a bony chest and a big belly, it is typically red or blue, with horns protruding from its head, tusks or fangs, and long claws on its hands and feet. It also sports a tiger-skin loincloth.

The Oni is considered to have an important role in Hell, tormenting the sinners as one of the wardens of the underworld. Supposedly an evil soul unable to be rehabilitated will become an Oni when they die. It is possible to transform into an Oni while still alive, but this is considered one of the worst punishments to ever be delivered, reserved for the nastiest people.

In modern times, the Oni have become more of a protective creature, losing their bad reputation and becoming good omens. People dressed as Oni often lead festival parades in order to bring good luck and dispel misfortune.

Should you find yourself in Japan, look up at the roofs of the buildings and you just might spot an Oni among the roof tiles. These are believed to ward off evil spirits, much like gargoyles in the West.

DAWN OF THE DOLLS

In Key West, Florida, lives one of the most terrifying toys in the world. Robert the Doll dates back to 1904 and was originally owned by the child of an eccentric artist. Robert wears a sailor suit, which many believe was an outfit his owner wore as an infant.

According to those who have worked and interacted with Robert, he has supernatural abilities that allow him to move his limbs and change his facial expressions. Horrifyingly, he has also been known to giggle, push figurines around the museum and demonstrate awareness of his surroundings and events nearby.

Those convinced of Robert's abilities believe he has caused a torrent of bad luck for those who have been anywhere near him, including car accidents, broken bones, divorce and job loss. People visiting him in the museum have reported unfortunate incidents directly afterward and have assumed that this is for "failing to respect" the doll.

PSYCHICS
AND
SPIRITUALISM

Channelling spirits and contacting the dead might not sound like your average Saturday night activity but at one point in history it was absolutely the norm. Two teenage girls who made contact with otherworldly spirits from their bedroom in upstate New York managed to kick-start one of the biggest religious movements of the nineteenth and twentieth centuries.

At its peak, ten per cent of Americans claimed to follow spiritualism, those who had lost loved ones turned to psychics as a matter of course and Ouija boards sold like hot cakes to become the family parlour game of the age. Public seances and spirit-led entertainment shows were all the rage, and Thomas Edison even tried to invent a spirit telephone to make communication with the dead a little easier.

Spiritualism's popularity had its ups and downs, but it notably – and perhaps quite understandably – peaked during times of great loss. Some estimates place the death count of the American Civil War – both soldiers and civilians – at as many as 1.5 million people. With so many Americans experiencing tumultuous grief, many turned to spiritualism as a means to making contact with loved ones lost in battle.

The First World War and the flu pandemic of 1918 also saw a take up in the movement, with anything up to 15 million killed globally in the former and the latter responsible for as many as an almost unfathomable 50 million deaths worldwide. People were desperate for word from their fathers, mothers, husbands, wives, siblings, children, aunts, uncles, grandparents and friends – they wanted to know that they had reached the next life. They wanted to know there was one.

It's also important to remember spiritualism first appeared in the 1840s at a time when the average life expectancy was around 50 years old, women regularly died in childbirth, children died in infancy and disease was more prevalent than today.

By the 1970s the movement had taken a dip in popularity – the finger of blame pointed by many at external factors such as the release of horror film The Exorcist, *which led many people to see Ouija boards as a gateway for demons. Nonetheless, spiritualism remains "alive" and well in many modern circles, boosted by a healthy crop of TV psychics touting their spiritual wares across the airwaves.*

PSYCHIC SISTERS

In mid-nineteenth century upstate New York, it's possible that a childhood prank gave rise to one of the greatest religious movements of the modern era.

In 1848, sisters Maggie and Kate Fox, aged 14 and 11 respectively, reported experiencing the paranormal in their house in Hydesville every night at bedtime. They claimed to have heard a series of knocks on the walls and furniture that they believed was communication from "the other side".

The sisters recounted their experience to a neighbour, who wanted to hear the knocking for herself. Maggie and Kate sat on their bed, while their mother, Margaret, spoke aloud: "Now count five," she said to the room. There were five loud knocks. She continued: "Now count fifteen." And the presence did what it was told. She then asked the presence to count the neighbour's age and thirty-three knocks followed. Margaret continued to question the presence. She asked it to knock three times if it was an injured spirit. It did so.

The date on which this occurred is significant – it was March 31, the eve of April Fool's Day, which many suspect prompted the sisters to set up an elaborate prank. Margaret was unaware of any potential tomfoolery and promptly moved the family out of the house, sending her daughters to live with their older sister, Leah, in nearby Rochester.

There was heightened public interest in the experiences of the Fox sisters, which historians believe is due to this area of New York State being alight with religious activity and reformation; both Mormonism and Seventh Day Adventism had taken root nearby. Two pillars of the community were intrigued and requested a demonstration at the Fox house. It was duly given, knocks were heard and older sister Leah displayed her own talents as a medium by communicating with the visitors' recently deceased daughter. This led to a public event in Rochester, which saw 400 attend to hear these "conversations" with the dead for themselves.

Well-regarded seer Andrew Jackson Davis invited the Fox sisters to his house to witness their talents first-hand. He was so moved by what he saw that, combined with the spiritual philosophies he had been practising, he began to tout their impressive medium abilities and this combination essentially gave rise to the spiritualist movement, propelling Davis into the position of leader and eventually causing him to be hailed the "John the Baptist of modern spiritualism".

Those who chose to follow spiritualism believed their lives could be enriched through communication with the dead, that insights from those who had passed on could help them to understand their eventual fate and that they had some say in their own salvation.

The Fox sisters travelled the country, communicating with the dead wherever they were welcome, and drew great crowds as well as commanding a pretty penny for personal seances. Sceptics would follow and study the sisters at work, but would reluctantly admit their talents remained a great mystery and could do nothing to disprove them.

The sisters' reign came to a head when, in 1888, Maggie addressed a large crowd and claimed that as children they had deceived people by using an apple attached to string to make the noises. Their method had evolved to using joints, knuckles and toes to make the sounds and she proceeded to demonstrate with her foot on a stool for all to see. She claimed Leah had exploited her younger sisters, knowing of the fraud all along.

Devoted spiritualists saw a way to press on, insisting that Maggie was a true medium, but her early work had been tainted by "other unseen intelligences". Maggie retracted her confession a year later, claiming her spirit guides had prompted a false admission. However, it was too late and she was rejected by the spiritualist community. She continued to give away "tricks of the trade" to those who would listen before she died in 1893, not long after her two sisters.

OUT OF THE CABINET

Another pair of siblings hailing from upstate New York with a definite hand in the rise of the spiritualist movement were the Davenport brothers.

While William and Ira Davenport were growing up in their family home in Buffalo, news of the Fox sisters' curious spiritual experiences intrigued their father. He was so interested in the connections the sisters were allegedly making with the next world that he decided to have a go himself.

The Davenports would sit around a table in their home and attempt to communicate with any spirits present. Upon recounting these would-be seances in later life, Ira claimed that on one occasion his younger sister Elizabeth levitated around the room.

The family decided it was William and Ira who possessed the ability to connect with spirits. Upon making contact with one that would become the family's spirit guide they were persuaded to take their talents out into the world. From beyond, John King supposedly told the family they should rent a hall within which the brothers could perform to the masses.

The early shows would see "tricks" similar to those performed by the Fox sisters, such as knocking and table-tipping. However, the Davenport shows quickly evolved to include musical instruments that floated in the air and played of their own accord, as well as spirit "hands" that pulled and prodded members of the audience.

The brothers were also the inventors of the spirit cabinet, which would go on to be used by many throughout the spiritualist movement. This consisted of what looked like a large closet with three compartments. The brothers would sit in their own compartment at opposite ends and would invite audience members to tie each of the brothers' hands together as tightly as they could before the cabinet doors were closed. Despite being tied up, music would play from the cabinet and hands would appear through holes in the walls, but when the doors were reopened the brothers' hands were still tied.

They certainly put on a show and offered more in the way of entertainment than the Fox sisters ever had. Occasionally an audience member would sit in the middle compartment of the cabinet and after the doors were closed would invariably find themselves thrown out of the box without their coat, perhaps with a necktie around their leg and a tambourine on their head. The doors to the brothers' compartments would be opened to find them sitting there quietly, hands tied up.

A dark seance was also part of their act, whereby the brothers were tied to their chairs or a table onstage and the lights were turned off. Ghostly forms would float around the stage, but when the lights were turned back on they were still tied securely to the furniture.

They were a sensation, and the spiritualist community widely accepted their abilities to communicate with those in the next world. The brothers never called themselves mediums, however, and preferred to let the audience decide the extent of their talents.

PSYCHICS AND SPIRITUALISM

They both believed they had a connection with the spirit world, but also later admitted to being very handy escapists. They took their role as entertainers seriously and went to great lengths to conceal the illusion from their adoring public, using accomplices and booby traps around the stage to avoid an invasion. In later life, Ira was befriended by legendary escape artist Harry Houdini who professed to having learned a lot from him.

REALIZING DREAMS

Manifestation is the practice of using your thoughts and energy to bring your aspirations into being. In short, those who use manifestation believe they can make their dreams and desires a reality through a variety of methods. These techniques involve focusing one's thoughts and energy on a particular goal, be that big or small, in order to communicate to the universe what is desired.

The guiding principle of manifestation is the "law of attraction" and many a celebrity claims to have used these techniques to attain success in their field. Notably, Oprah Winfrey believes we can all use the power of our thoughts to manifest a different reality, and that "letting go" of her disappointment following her audition for *The Color Purple* saw her offered the part two months later.

Jim Carrey, one of the highest-paid actors in the world, is another celebrity who swears his manifestation practice got him to where he is today. He claims when he was starting out and had no money, he would use the power of his mind to visualize directors being interested in his talent and praising him. He also wrote himself a $10 million cheque and dated it five years in the future, carrying it in his wallet and looking at it often. Just before the five years was up he found out his part in *Dumb and Dumber* was going to earn him $10 million.

Arnold Schwarzenegger, Jay-Z, Lady Gaga and Will Smith are also big believers in manifestation.

SCOTLAND'S LAST "WITCH"

In 1944, spiritualist Helen Duncan was the last person in Britain to be tried and sentenced under the Witchcraft Act 1735. A clairvoyant who progressed to become a more physical or "trance" medium, Duncan travelled the length of the country from her native Scotland to hold regular seances and communicate with clients' loved ones who had passed on.

She would purportedly produce the form of the dead by emitting ectoplasm from her mouth. In spiritualism, ectoplasm refers to a substance or spiritual energy produced by trance mediums – the substance is often described as viscous, but in Duncan's practice it was "cloud-like". It was claimed she could summon people's relatives and they would actually appear, talk to and touch their relatives.

During one seance in 1941, Duncan communicated with a dead sailor from HMS *Barham*, revealing to her audience that the ship had been wrecked in the Mediterranean. This was factually true, but not common knowledge at the time, with the British government keeping the disaster under wraps – almost 900 British naval officers had died from a German torpedo strike. It's safe to say the establishment kept an eye on her from then on.

In 1944, prior to the planned top-secret Normandy D-Day landings, in a fit of paranoia that she might give the game away, one of Duncan's seances was raided by the police. There was a scuffle as the officers physically restrained her and tried to stop the ectoplasm from exiting her mouth.

She was arrested and put on trial at the Old Bailey. The Witchcraft Act 1735 had not been used for over a hundred years, but it was under this legislation that Duncan was sentenced to nine months at London's Holloway Prison. She became the last person to be prosecuted under the Act and in 1951 it was repealed and replaced with the Fraudulent Mediums Act 1951, which prohibited anyone from deceptively claiming to be a psychic and profiting from it. If psychic activity was all about entertainment with no financial reward, that was just fine. It is intriguing to note that in the same year spiritualism was legally recognized in the UK as a religion. The Fraudulent Mediums Act was in turn repealed in 2008.

Duncan was released from prison the same year of her arrest but was continually harassed – her seances regularly raided in an attempt to prove she was a fraud. She died in 1956. Her Scottish hometown of Callander was presented with a bronze bust of her likeness, but it seems even in the present day Duncan divides opinion, so it was taken in by the Stirling Smith Art Gallery and Museum in Stirling for safekeeping.

SPIRITS SAY "CHEESE"

As spiritualism gathered pace following the US national trauma of the Civil War, photographers were seemingly able to capture the images of loved ones who had passed on.

The emergence of these photographs caused a media sensation and soon everybody wanted one. The most famous example is of Mary Todd Lincoln with a ghostly impression of her departed husband President Abraham Lincoln standing behind her.

However, not everyone was convinced. Photographers were found to have used methods involving double exposures to create the illusion of a ghostly figure – specifically the person whom their client had requested appear in the picture. In an era when spiritualism was incredibly popular and around ten per cent of Americans were believers in the movement, it was considered cruel – criminal even – to play with followers' emotions.

EDISON'S DIRECT LINE

In 1877, Thomas Edison invented the phonograph and created the first ever sound recording that could be played back. The very first words to ever be recorded were: "Mary had a little lamb. Its fleece was white as snow. And everywhere that Mary went, the lamb was sure to go." Often referred to as a "talking machine", Edison's first phonograph was simple and recordings on tin foil could only be played back a handful of times, but everyone went wild for his new invention and were excited by the possibilities it offered.

By 1920, Edison had honed his phonograph into something far more user-friendly and announced that he was working on a new machine that would allow people to contact the dead – a "spirit phone" of sorts to connect with the afterlife.

Edison was interested in the spiritualist movement – it had grown in popularity during the First World War, picking up many new recruits – and his interest lay in demonstrating that science was the way to connect with the spirit world. He said, "the methods and apparatus commonly used and discussed are just a lot of unscientific nonsense".

Deeming Ouija boards and other tools used by mediums to be clunky and inaccurate, he believed any physical power possessed by those in the afterlife was likely to be "extremely slight" and that any instrument that might enable communication between this life and the next should be "super delicate – as finely responsive as human ingenuity can make it". He also felt that such a machine should be able to record any interaction with those beyond the grave.

Edison carried out a secret demonstration of his spiritual work in progress in his lab, with several scientists invited to see what he had achieved. In 1933, two years after Edison's death, *Modern Mechanix* magazine reported on details of the demo that had come to light: "Edison set up a photo-electric cell. A tiny pencil of light, coming from a powerful lamp, bored through the darkness and struck the active surface of this cell, where it was transformed instantly into a feeble electric current. Any object, no matter how thin, transparent or small, would cause a registration on the cell if it cut through the beam."

The scientists present apparently spent a number of hours watching closely for any sign of movement, signifying a connection with the world beyond, but unfortunately there was none. Edison continued to work on his spirit phone, keen to prove that science would prevail, but sadly he never succeeded. Nonetheless, this did not dent many Americans' continued belief in the possibility of spiritual contact.

HOLD THE SPACELINE

In the early 1900s, as spiritualism steadily gathered followers, an American medium practising under the pseudonym Vesta la Viesta claimed to have communicated with beings from elsewhere in the galaxy.

Through astral projection – an out-of-body experience in which one's soul leaves one's body – she claimed to have made contact with inhabitants of Mars and Venus. She gave many well-attended lectures about her experiences of astral travel, her audience fascinated to gain insight of life beyond Earth.

She described Martian architecture as "transcendent" and said their culture, society and systems of government were of a similar nature to those on Earth. As reported in the *Rock Island Argus* in 1904, to one audience she described:

> ... *an enthusiastic, stalwart, noble race of men, with complexions shiny and black as ebony. They are wiry, muscular, taught and very supple. They play with electricity as we would with fireworks. They have a way of flashing firelike radiations from their legs that makes their presence decidedly luminous, lively and at times somewhat dazzling. They appear like huge warriors attired in atmospheric raiments of flame.*

Martian women she described as "beautiful, with daintily molded forms and with very fair complexions. Their flesh is luminous."

She claimed Venus to be a "small but very beautiful and tropical planet" inhabited by "a charming race of beings". She continued:

> *They are associated most happily in soul mated couples, for they have a flexible astral or psychological tubing which invisibly connects their bodies and prevents them from wandering or straying or being separated at any time from their soul mate.*

The detail was startling and her followers were hungry for more. In 1907, after two years of silence, she spoke of an astral voyage to Neptune, claiming to have been taught about a new form of love that existed on the planet. She described a "soul kiss", which involved the arousal of the nervous system, cellular breathing (through the pores of the skin) and the "wireless" transmission of love that could travel "through mountains and over seas" and last for hours. As reported in the *Spokane Press*, she said:

> *When you have been properly developed and try on the soul kiss, your whole being responds to a perfect delirium of ecstasy. It is like the fusing of two great forces when responsive souls meet in this exercise.*

She was so moved by her experience that she penned a song about it called "Description of a Soul Kiss", the lyrics taking the listener further into the realms of this new form of love, claiming the kiss to have "opened wide all the closed up avenues of my soul", closing with "the fairies have transported us to their love paradise center, uniting our souls with a kiss!"

ROYAL GRIEF

Queen Victoria turned to spiritualism in the 1860s following the death of her husband Prince Albert. Overcome with grief, she entered her "mourning period", which saw her dress in black clothing and wear sombre jewellery containing locks of her dead husband's hair until she died in 1901.

Many were suspicious when 13-year-old medium Robert Lees got word to Victoria of his contact with Albert during a seance, alleging the prince had wanted to convey a message to her. However, when Victoria summoned Lees to Buckingham Palace he seemingly communicated with Albert and relayed information he likely could not have known – such as pet names they had for each other.

Lees performed many seances for Victoria at the palace, as did others with their finger on the pulse of the spiritual world. The Queen took a great interest in spiritualism and even apparently sought her deceased husband's advice on political matters.

TOOLS OF THE SPIRIT TRADE

A product of the popularity of the spiritualist movement when it was first conceived in the 1890s, the Ouija board – also known as a spirit or talking board – was only used in parlour games and private houses. It was even sold in toy shops and touted as a game for the whole family. Advertisements attempting to lure would-be customers talked of a magical device that would answer questions about the past, present and future "with marvellous accuracy", linking "the known, unknown, the material and immaterial". And, remarkably, it was proven to work at the Patent Office, with toy manufacturer the Kennard Novelty Company granted the first patent.

The board hasn't changed much in the past 130 years – other than that the early boards were wooden, and these days are more likely to be cardboard. Featuring, as it always has, the alphabet, numbers 0–9, the words "yes" and "no", and occasionally "hello" and "goodbye". An accompanying planchette (French for "little plank"), a heart-shaped pointer upon which the conductor of the Ouija board would place their fingers was also integral to the art.

Participants would place their fingers on the planchette and, while asking questions, allow it to be guided toward letters and numbers in order to spell out and communicate a message. Seemingly – and incredibly – Kennard had asked the as-yet-unnamed prototype board what they should call it – the board answered "ouija" and when they asked what it meant it answered, "good luck".

In the early 1900s the board was popularized as a tool for divination and making serious contact with the spirit world. With communication with the dead really quite common at this time, before the invention of the Ouija board participants in a seance would be forced to call out each letter of the alphabet and wait for a knock at the right letter. It was all very time-consuming. The new spirit board offered a fibre-optic broadband connection to the spirit world compared with the dial-up method of old, and for that it was hugely popular.

Along with this hotline to the world beyond, came tales reported in the press of Ouija board users obeying the messages they were receiving. One woman claimed she had received a message using her spirit board to leave her mother's dead body in her armchair for 15 days, rather than reporting it to the authorities, and then burying her in the backyard. Two women confessed to murdering someone, alleging the spirits told them to do it. Others joined the army on their advice and wrote Ouija spirits into their will, leaving them vast sums of money.

The board continued to soar in popularity and in 1944, when many US service people were being killed in the Second World War, over the course of five months one New York department store sold 50,000 of them. In 1967, two million boards were sold – outselling Monopoly.

It wasn't to last. The 1973 film *The Exorcist* told the story of a possessed 12-year-old who, after playing with a Ouija board, projectile vomited green gunge and found her head spinning 360 degrees, among all sorts of ungodly behaviour.

PSYCHICS AND SPIRITUALISM

No longer a tool for harmless fun or communication with gentle souls from beyond, the boards became associated with the Devil. People began to believe that the risk was too great of accidentally contacting a demon and getting themselves possessed. Ouija boards started cropping up in horror films, portrayed as a sinister pastime and a bad rep took root.

WORD FROM THE OTHER SIDE

These days, people are more familiar with a planchette referring to the pointer used on a Ouija board to spell out a message, but earlier models in the second half of the 1800s were precursors to the Ouija board, designed to convey messages from the spirit world.

The planchette was a flat, heart-shaped piece of wood with two wheeled legs at the wider end and a holder for a pencil at the narrower end. When the pencil was in the holder, the planchette would be placed on a piece of paper and, much like the Ouija format, people would ask it questions.

Through what people referred to as "automatic writing", the planchette would then scrawl out communication from whomever or whatever had been contacted. These devices were wildly popular in the 1860s and manufacturers produced versions in a variety of shapes and sizes, claiming some materials were more suited to spirit connection than others as competition grew. Some also offered attachments that would supposedly protect the planchette and its user from evil spirits, should any find their way through.

SPIRIT MIRROR TEACHINGS

Court astrologer to Queen Elizabeth I, John Dee claimed to have a divine connection with both angels and spirits. Dee was a respected astronomer, mathematician, magician and expert in global navigation. He held a great interest in the supernatural and it was often proposed he made no distinctions between his pursuits in this world and his scientific research.

In later life, Dee would concentrate all his efforts on communicating with the spirit world, using tools such as a crystal ball and spirit mirror. Working with renowned medium Edward Kelley, the two men claimed to summon angels and spirits to the surface of these objects through the practice of "scrying" – the process of gazing in the hope of making a connection with an otherworldly presence.

Dee spent the last 30 years of his life dedicated to scrying – what he referred to as "actions with spirits" on a mission to "learn the universal language of creation". He documented every interaction he had over three decades, learning from the angels a new language in which he wrote extensively as they dictated to him. He supposedly communicated with the angels that ruled the seven planetary spheres – identifying them by their individual names and titles – and through these meetings and teachings had ultimately hoped to heal the rift he saw between God and man. These writings were recorded in secret and only discovered long after Dee's death.

THE ORIGINAL GHOSTWRITER

In 1916, in St Louis, Missouri, housewife Pearl Curran claimed she had contacted the spirit of a seventeenth-century English woman named Patience Worth, who was dictating poems and stories to her via her Ouija board.

Curran was not a medium, nor did she have a great interest in spiritualism, she was merely a dabbler with the Ouija board – as many were at the time. She and friend Emily Hutchings would take tea together each afternoon and occasionally play with the spirit board. Neither were that enamoured with it as they only managed to obtain gibberish, until one day a message came through loud and clear: "Many moons ago I lived. Again I come. My name is Patience Worth."

The spirit spoke to them in archaic language, using "thee" and "thou" and was reluctant to answer questions about herself, claiming: "About me you know too much. Yesterday is dead. Let my mind rest as to the past." Worth was keen to convey other things and had no time for chit-chat.

Curran started to use her spirit board more and more often, intrigued as she was by Worth's messages and their apparent ability to contact her every time. The communication grew in its frequency, Curran finding that Worth had a lot to say and had chosen her as the conduit. The messages came through so fast that Curran found herself unable to write them all down and eventually found that the words – along with the images – were being transmitted to her mind and she was able to dictate them to someone else to write down.

The images of seventeenth-century English life were so vivid she was able to describe items and aspects of life, clothing and kitchen implements, sounds and smells of places and times she had never previously visited. They baffled those who wanted to cry "hoax".

Over the course of 25 years, Worth dictated around 400,000 words from beyond the grave. Among these were, extraordinarily, some 5,000 poems, a play, countless short stories and several novels, which were published to critical acclaim. The naysayers were similarly baffled by this prolific outpouring of material. Curran was a woman of limited education, not a big reader, and had little or no knowledge of the language that was being used or the historic period from which it hailed.

She was more than happy to let interested parties sit in on these writing sessions – and many did, intrigued at the woman who could channel a dead writer with much to say.

As time wore on, Worth became impatient with her host – often speaking in a condescending manner to her when she failed to grasp the meaning of words being conveyed. Their connection began to deteriorate and eventually stopped altogether. Curran was frequently accused of using Worth as a bizarre and attention-seeking publicity stunt to promote her own literary output and accrue fame.

Pearl Curran died in 1937 and her obituary in the paper was headlined: "Patience Worth is dead."

LINCOLN'S VISION

First lady to President Abraham Lincoln, Mary Todd Lincoln had a strong belief in spiritualism and the supernatural. The couple had four sons, but only one made it to adulthood, which led Mary Todd to spiritualism in order to contact them all. Lincoln somewhat reluctantly followed her down that path, always viewing the practices with a dose of scepticism.

Lincoln also claimed to have seen suggestions of his own death on more than one occasion – soon after his election glimpsing a double image of his face reflected in a mirror, one his real face and the other a ghostly imitation. On another occasion, in a dream recorded by his ward after the president recounted it to him:

There seemed to be a death-like stillness about me. Then I heard subdued sobs, as if a number of people were weeping. I thought I left my bed and wandered downstairs. I arrived at the East Room. Before me was a catafalque, on which rested a corpse wrapped in funeral vestments. Around it were stationed soldiers who were acting as guards; and there was a throng of people, some gazing mournfully upon the corpse, whose face was covered, others weeping pitifully. "Who is dead in the White House?" I demanded of one of the soldiers. "The President," was his answer. "He was killed by an assassin."

Todd held many seances in the White House in a bid to reach her lost children and cope with her grief. When Abraham Lincoln was assassinated in 1865 – shot in the head by John Wilkes Booth while watching a play at Ford's Theatre in Washington DC – she turned the focus of her seances to her dead husband.

THE SPIRITS ALWAYS SHINE ON TV

While in modern times spiritualist practices can be found at play all over the world, it has to be said that – perhaps unsurprisingly – America commercializes them like nowhere else.

Enter the TV psychic – those who drum up interest via talk shows and YouTube, and go on to tour the country appearing to audiences of hundreds, maybe more, and charging high ticket prices. To the believer or to the interested it's worth every penny.

Tyler Henry is a Generation Z TV medium who states he realized he had psychic abilities at the age of 10 after his grandmother passed away. In high school he gave readings to staff and students and at the age of 19, after appearing on *Keeping Up with the Kardashians* where he performed a reading for one of the sisters, he snagged his own TV show – *Hollywood Medium with Tyler Henry*. On it he gives readings to celebrities and contacts a deceased loved one of their choosing. So far he has given the psychic treatment to RuPaul, Rebel Wilson, Megan Fox and Kylie Jenner, among countless other celebrities. Most who take part are reduced to tears at some point or another.

Naysayers have accused the young clairvoyant of researching his subjects' backgrounds, but Tyler insists he doesn't know who he will be reading until he arrives at their house. The subjects also admit that the intimate details he discovers are often so personal to them there's no way he could have sought them out elsewhere.

Miss Cleo, a medium whose services were advertised on TV, worked for the Psychic Readers Network in the late 1990s and 2000s, also making appearances on US talk shows. Along with conducting tarot readings, during TV appearances she would allow audience members to ask a fairly general question such as "Should I move cities?" or "What do you see happening in my career?" After taking the questioner's date of birth she would then matter-of-factly tell them what was going to happen and, in some cases, give them orders about what they should and shouldn't do.

Theresa Caputo's show *Long Island Medium* sees her break through to the other side for many an emotional participant, often with a tragic tale to be told about the person they are trying to contact. A world away from *Hollywood Medium*, Caputo scouts around her native Long Island supposedly randomly selecting people in cafés and shops and passing on messages from lost loved ones. With her striking towering hairdo, claw-like false nails and relentless (as possible) optimism, TV psychic fans find her refreshing and perhaps more believable than others.

THE ARTISTS' MEDIUM

In mid-Victorian England, Georgina Houghton was honing her skills as an artistic medium. She had become interested in the spiritualist movement following the death of her sister and began to attend seances in order to communicate with her from one world to the next.

Throughout the 1860s and 70s, Houghton would paint in a trance-like state and profess that she was channelling great artists such as Titian and Correggio through her mortal paintbrush. Over the years, she produced hundreds of abstract paintings created in this manner and was not alone – the world of "spirit art" seemingly very much alive and thriving in Britain at the time.

Practising spiritualists saw these paintings as proof for non-believers that the worlds of the living and dead could communicate with each other and could supposedly interpret the artworks in a way that those outside the movement could not.

Naturally, the public was divided on the matter of art created by and attributed to the spirits of dead artists and the genre was largely forgotten until more recent times when several exhibitions featuring spirit paintings have taken place in major London galleries.

SUMMONING SHAMANS

Shamanism is practised in many parts of the world today, but its origins are in northern Europe and parts of northern Asia. This religious practice is headed up by a shaman, who followers believe interacts with spirits by reaching an altered state of consciousness. The shaman's goal is to guide these spiritual energies into the world of the living – usually for healing purposes, although the spirits can be called upon to help with other things too.

Historically, shamanism is associated with indigenous and tribal societies. It predates all organized religion and is believed to have originated as far back as the Paleolithic period. Followers believe a shaman is chosen for their abilities to connect with a world beyond our own and are afforded the power to heal the sick and help to escort souls of the dead to the afterlife.

As with many religions, shamanism varies throughout the world, but they share common beliefs, notably the existence of spirits and the importance placed on the role they play in the lives of individuals as well as wider human society. Followers believe spirits can be benevolent or malevolent, and that a true shaman will have the ability to treat illness caused by malevolent spirits.

PSYCHICS AND SPIRITUALISM

Shamans are a talented bunch, able to achieve a trance-like state and go on successful "vision quests", a ritual involving fasting in nature to induce a kind of visionary ecstasy in order to find answers to life's many questions. Vision quests – which go by many names – are a rite of passage in some cultures, with those approaching adulthood taking part in a succession of ceremonies involving fasting and praying to the spirit world, the goal being to achieve dreams or visions that will then be interpreted by elders.

It is also believed that a shaman's spirit has the ability to leave their body in order to seek answers in the spirit world. As well as performing ceremonies involving throwing bones and runes, they are able to evoke spirit guides in the forms of animals.

Along with spiritual healing, shamans will have a thorough understanding of local plant life and their healing properties and will prescribe complementary herbal treatments. A shaman can also allow their spirit to enter the patient's body in order to square up to the malevolent or infections spirit.

One with shamanic talents usually commands great respect, power and prestige among their community; and the job is not without risk – with many a plant poisonous and at worst fatal if used incorrectly.

SUPERNATURAL SOUNDS

British composer, pianist and spirit medium Rosemary Brown caused a media sensation in the 1970s when she claimed dead composers were channelling their new masterpieces through her.

Brown alleged to come from a family of psychics and had been communicating with dead musicians from a very early age, when at the age of seven – in 1923 – she received a visit from a spirit with long white hair, who told her she would find fame as a musician one day and he would help her to get there. A decade later she saw a photograph of Hungarian composer Franz Liszt and recognized him as the spirit who had appeared to her.

In 1964, Brown claimed Liszt had appeared to her once more and she began to produce pieces of music purportedly dictated to her by long-dead composers including Brahms, Bach, Chopin, Schubert, Rachmaninoff, Beethoven and Mozart, among others. Within these works were supposedly a 40-page sonata from Schubert, two sonatas and two symphonies from Beethoven and a piece in three movements from Chopin.

She also claimed each composer had a different method of communicating their creations to her, with Bach and Beethoven dictating the notes; Liszt controlling her hands; Chopin telling her the notes and guiding her fingers to the correct keys; and Schubert singing the notes to her.

PEN TO PAPER

Jane Roberts was another woman who apparently found herself being channelled by a spiritual being who was using her mortal body to create art.

Born in that hotbed of spiritual activity, upstate New York in the 1920s, Roberts went on to produce written material that is often referred to as one of the cornerstones of New Age philosophy. She was a prolific writer and produced numerous works of poetry, as well as children's fiction, science fiction and fantasy novels, non-fiction and a plethora of short stories.

She and her husband also liked to dabble with a Ouija board and she had written a book about extra-sensory perception. Through the spirit board they had made contact with a spirit called Seth, who spoke to them regularly through the board and eventually began channelling straight into Roberts' mind.

In 1963, Roberts claimed she was sat at her desk about to write poetry, when "a fantastic avalanche of radical new ideas burst into my head with tremendous force". She said, "it was as if the physical world were really tissue-paper thin, hiding infinite dimensions of reality, and I was flung through the tissue paper with a huge ripping sound." When she regained composure, she found she had scrawled many notes and given them a title – "The physical universe as idea construction".

Over the next six years she allowed Seth to project his teachings through her body. He was, according to Roberts, "an energy personality essence no longer focused in physical matter". His voice through Roberts was deeper and his tone could be both stern and jovial.

In 1969 she published *The Seth Material*, a collection of the writings gained through his insights. His teachings were spiritual – theorizing that consciousness creates matter, and that the individual can create their own reality through thought and expectation – much like the practice of manifestation.

Roberts continued to hold trance sessions right up to her death in 1984, where she would dictate Seth's words for her husband to write down. It's estimated she performed a massive 1,500 of these sessions and some of them were to an audience. In total she wrote ten volumes of these "Seth books" and claimed her role in their inception was merely as a medium.

ELEMENTARY, DEAR PHANTOMS

Creator of Sherlock Holmes Arthur Conan Doyle was one of the most ardent spiritualists of his era. He was initially a sceptic, but upon attending a seance in 1880 that all changed. Doyle claimed to have received a message from his son, who had died of pneumonia following battle injuries during the First World War. So convinced was he of mortals' ability to communicate with the spirit world that he toured Europe and America specifically to preach the word of spiritualism and what lay beyond this life.

Doyle struck up an unlikely friendship with magician and famous escape artist Harry Houdini. The men were united by their shared intrigue of spiritualism. Houdini was desperate to communicate with his dead mother, but despite his interest in spiritualism was also sceptical about it. He was a showman, a magician, making a living from entertainment through trickery and had been known in the early days of his career to fake a seance or two in order to pay the bills.

Houdini set about exposing fraudulent mediums, claiming them to be "human leeches". Doyle was not impressed and the final nail in the coffin of their friendship came when Houdini attended a seance at the Doyles' house in which they claimed to produce multiple pages of "automatic writing" from the spirit of Houdini's mother. Houdini went on record to say he disputed the Doyles' claim of communication with his ma, saying it was far too grammatically accurate and that her written English had been terrible.

CROSS YOUR PALM

Also known as "chiromancy", palmistry, or palm reading, is one of the most highly regarded forms of divination. Dating back to the ancient world, the practice involves analysing the lines across the hands and palms in order to gain an insight into what lies in the owner's future.

A palm-reader studies both the left and right hands, and as well as reading the lines also makes observations pertaining to the shape of the hands, texture of the skin, and quality and cleanliness of the fingernails.

There are four different hand shapes – earth, fire, air and water – and the fleshy areas of the palms known as "mounts" and "plains" are related to various different life themes.

The Mount of Jupiter at the base of the index finger represents ambition, confidence and leadership; the Mount of Saturn at the base of the middle finger symbolizes fortitude, responsibility and wisdom; the Mount of Apollo at the base of the ring finger corresponds to essence, optimism and vitality; the Mount of Mercury at the base of the little finger represents communication and intelligence; the Mount of Luna at the bottom of the palm beneath the little finger symbolizes imagination, intuition and psychic powers;

and the Mount of Venus at the base of the thumb looks to attraction, love and sensuality.

Mars is important in palmistry, with Inner Mars, Outer Mars and the Plain of Mars covering many themes. Inner – or Lower – Mars can be found in between the thumb and index finger and represents physical strength and tenacity; Outer – or Upper – Mars symbolizes emotional bravery and perseverance; while the Plain of Mars in the lower centre of the palm shows how the qualities related to Inner and Outer Mars are balanced.

Then there are the lines themselves – the head line, life line, heart line, sun line and fate line. These folds and creases vary from person to person, and supposedly go a long way in helping a reader to determine certain aspects of one's future.

While it has its fair share of loyal believers, in more recent times palmistry is often seen as a fairground attraction, claiming to offer those being read a chance to shine a light on potential opportunities that lie ahead.

Key to the modern palmistry movement, during the 1800s and early 1900s, Irishman William Warner – better known by his palm-reading pseudonym Cheiro – enjoyed a large following and attracted various celebrities of the age keen to have their fortune told. Various Americans and Europeans flocked to him, including Mata Hari, Oscar Wilde, the Prince of Wales (later Edward VIII), US president Grover Cleveland and Mark Twain. Twain had been a sceptic of the fashionable practice, but visited Cheiro nonetheless. He wrote in his visitors' book: "Cheiro has exposed my character to me with humiliating accuracy. I ought not to confess this accuracy, still I am moved to do so."

WITCHCRAFT AND THE OCCULT

Witchcraft has had a turbulent history for centuries, with accusations flung at more innocent victims than one can bear to count. Aside from the more notorious witch trials are the lesser-known cases, but just as brutal in terms of torture and loss of life. Spare a thought for the witches on Halloween – they were not all purveyors of the dark arts, with some using their forces for good and others falsely accused with no evidence of any sorcery.

The world of witchcraft is associated with much death, despair and oppression, especially from the late 1500s onward – an era that saw the persecution, imprisonment and execution of up to 200,000 suspected witches across Europe, some of whom had no connections with sorcery whatsoever and 90 per cent of whom were women.

With witchcraft the buzzword of the time, people were terrified of powers they didn't understand and blamed the practice for pretty much everything that went wrong in their lives. This meant the nearest woman was often blamed, thrown in jail, put on trial and, more often than not, executed – sometimes simply for glancing at a horse one day only for it to die a week later. It's hard for us today to understand this thought process.

James I, king of Scotland and then England, was weirdly obsessed with the occult and wrote a book entitled Daemonologie, *which explored at length the dark arts. His fascination led to him pushing through Parliament the Witchcraft Statute of 1604 making the crime of witchcraft punishable by death.*

Along with his desire to change England for the better, the king's fascination was likely based on anxieties about what this mysterious magical world was capable of. The nervousness trickled into the public consciousness and took root deeply over the decades that followed.

On these pages you will meet the tyrannical witchfinders who were devoid of mercy and often had a financial agenda persecuting those practising so-called black magic. Other figures – both from history and legend – who dabbled in the dark arts will come to light, and we'll look at the importance of potions and poppets in this mysterious world.

MERLIN OF MANY TALENTS

Possibly the most famous wizard of all before Harry Potter made an entrance, Merlin first appeared in Welsh folklore in the 1100s. Traditionally, the story goes that Merlin was born a cambion – the product of the mating of human and demon, which explains his supernatural abilities. In Merlin's case, these powers fell into the realms of soothsaying and shape-shifting.

His tale, as first documented by cleric and historian Geoffrey of Monmouth, is credited with bridging the gap between the worlds of Christianity and Paganism. And given Merlin's impressive resumé of prophecy and magic, it's unsurprising that King Arthur and his father before him would want to choose this wise wizard as a mentor and adviser.

The story of Merlin is thought by many to have been based on someone real, perhaps Merddyn Wyllt (Merlin the Wild), who hailed from either Wales or Scotland around the sixth century.

Ever since then hundreds upon hundreds, if not thousands, of works of fiction have been created with Merlin and King Arthur as central characters. Historians dedicating their life's work to Merlin are numerous, and in more recent times there have been countless TV and film adaptations, with a long list of talent stepping up to tackle the role.

Merlin experts are convinced some of his foresights (or perhaps these were more likely to be Geoffrey's...) predicted events centuries before they occurred. Despite Merlin's dominant presence in literature, in the late Middle Ages as the Welsh and English grew more nervous about anything associated with witchcraft, depictions of him were either less favourable or in some narratives he was swiftly killed off in an unpleasant manner. Mark Twain even portrayed him as a villain in his 1889 novel *A Connecticut Yankee in King Arthur's Court*.

The most famous oft-told story to include Merlin's demise "The Lady of the Lake", in which Merlin becomes infatuated with an aquatic enchantress who grants King Arthur the gift of the magic sword Excalibur. One version of the story has the lady embark on a romantic relationship with Merlin, locking him in a tower and visiting him regularly to have her way with him. At the end she seals him in a tomb where he dies a slow death.

One could spend a lifetime consuming the stories of Merlin, there are so many – and some do. Whether the stories of Merlin, King Arthur and the Knights of the Round Table have any roots in reality is up for debate, but there are thousands upon thousands out there who would relish having that debate with you.

ASIAN WITCHCRAFT

The stark differences between occult traditions and beliefs across the globe are both striking and fascinating.

In Japanese legend, witches are separated into two categories according to their familiar – snakes and foxes. The most common in Japanese folklore is the witch who employs a fox. The fox is originally bribed with its favourite foods, before the witch strikes a deal with it, offering food and shelter in return for magical services. Japanese legend, much like in Western tradition, states the fox is sly, with the ability to shape-shift. Foxes have been known to disguise themselves as women to trap men; and when a fox becomes a man's familiar it is said to become a force of extreme evil.

Central Asian folklore posits that if a witch murders someone they then own the soul of their victim. And magic has been a big part of Chinese life and traditions for centuries, intersecting with religion and widely accepted throughout society.

Sadly, witchcraft persecution still happens in some parts of India, despite witch-hunting being banned in the mid nineteenth century. Those accused face horrendous abuse and even death, and if they are lucky enough to escape are likely to be ostracized from their community.

THE WITCHFINDER-GENERAL'S PAYDAY

In 1645, lawyer Matthew Hopkins was appointed England's Witchfinder General and saw it as his mission to destroy anything associated with "works of the Devil". He claimed to have been officially commissioned by Parliament – but there is no evidence he was – and set out to expose and prosecute anyone associated with witchcraft. Along with his crew of creepily named "lady pickers", he visited the towns and villages of eastern England to hound those who practised the so-called "black arts". Methods of torture used on suspected witches included keeping them awake for days on end until they were so sleep deprived they would have admitted to doing anything at all; cutting them with a knife and if they didn't bleed they were a witch (Hopkins' entourage took to using blunt or retractable blades); and binding the limbs of the accused to a chair and throwing them into the nearest body of water (if they sank, they drowned and if they floated they would be tried as a witch and most probably executed).

Hopkins was paid handsomely on commission, so as far as he was concerned the more witches he could convict the better. Over the course of just two years he is suspected to have been responsible for the deaths of as many as 400 women. In terms of financial reward for his services, it's likely he collected around £1,000 – in an era when a farm worker's wage was around 6 pence a day.

Women were accused of bewitching people who had fallen ill; killing livestock that happened to die close to where they lived; the death of sickly newborns; miscarriage; raising storms that wrecked ships; fraternizing with imps; communicating with the Devil in animal form; murder by malicious thought – and the list goes on.

Women who had indeed turned to witchcraft often did so in a bid to escape poverty – a deal with the Devil said to afford them material gain. The women put on trial were rarely spared, instead being sentenced to death by hanging. During the seventeenth century, 68 were killed in Bury St Edmunds, Suffolk, with 18 hanged in a single day in Chelmsford, Essex.

Hopkins published his book *A Discovery of Witches* in 1647, detailing his cruel methods and punishments, and died of tuberculosis that same year aged 27. According to historian Malcolm Gaskill, Hopkins "lives on as an anti-hero and bogeyman – utterly ethereal, endlessly malleable".

PICK UP A POPPET

Poppets, or dolls, have been used in folk magic and witchcraft for centuries, and their history goes back even further than that – it's thought that the oldest dolls discovered by archaeologists were unlikely to have belonged to children, instead used for religious or ritualistic purposes.

Magical dolls can be constructed from anything; from cloth, wood, wax, clay, corn husks, sticks or potatoes, and are usually formed to represent the subject upon which a spell is being cast or the person who needs a helping hand on their magical journey.

In Scandinavia poppets are used in the home as "kitchen witches" – placed in the kitchen to bring good luck and ward off bad spirits. Elsewhere in Europe, pagan traditions saw "corn dollies" and "corn mothers" created from straw at harvest time in a bid to accommodate the spirit of the corn, which they believed was rendered homeless with the cutting of the crop.

The fairy or angel placed atop your Christmas tree is rooted in this practice, the theory being it will guard your home and bring enchantment into your house throughout the winter.

Poppets fall into the realm of "image magic", which in ancient witchcraft is even said to include cave paintings and spells that require an effigy to be moulded from mud or clay.

WHITE WITCH OF SURREY

Nestled into the sandstone cliff of the Wey Valley at Moor Park near Farnham in Surrey, UK, you'll find the cave of white witch Mother Ludlam.

So the story goes, Mother Ludlam lived in the cave in the 1600s and was an old, friendly witch who liked to help out in the community. Villagers knew her as a kind woman who would lend anyone anything they asked for, on the understanding that it must be returned within two days – or else.

Villagers would stand atop a rock outside her cave and make their request, before heading home where they would find the item on their doorstep – what service. As long as the item was returned within two days everyone was happy.

One day a man visited Mother Ludlam and asked to borrow her cauldron. She was hesitant but had a reputation to uphold and so agreed he could borrow it for the standard two days. However, the man foolishly held on to the cauldron and Mother Ludlam took a rare outing from the cave to track him down. Upon hearing she was on the hunt for him, the bad borrower sought refuge in Frensham Church and took the cauldron with him. Should you visit the church today you will see the cauldron – or at least a cauldron – there. Locals find it a bizarre addition to the religious building, but the fact that it was also used for hundreds of years by local priests in need of a vessel for their homebrew only adds to the allure of the story.

Another version of the legend of Mother Ludlam sees her recognizing the cauldron borrower as the Devil after spotting his hooved footprints at the cave entrance and refusing to lend her prized cooking pot. He stole it anyway and ran off. As he made his escape, so fable has it, he took great leaps and every time he landed he formed a hill – these hills are known today as the Devil's Jumps. He allegedly dropped the cauldron (also known as a "kettle") on what is today known as Kettlebury Hill. She then put the cauldron in the church for safekeeping so the Devil couldn't reach it.

HANDY GUIDE TO WITCHCRAFT

Originally composed in Arabic in the eleventh century, *Picatrix* is the modern name for what is often described as a "handbook of talismanic magic". Its Arabic title translating as "The Aim of the Sage" or "The Goal of the Wise", this 400-page book fuses older works on magic and astrology and is a remarkably thorough account of old celestial magic. It was considered such a useful magical reference text that centuries ago it was translated into Spanish and Latin.

Widely hailed as one of the most important records of medieval and Renaissance magic, its contents span Hermetic magical philosophy, ritual, talismanic and natural magic. The focus on astrology in understanding life and the universe's planetary forces is deeply rooted in the text, along with the trinity of matter, spirit and divinity. Then there are, of course, a whole load of spells. These are apparently incredibly complex, not for beginners and require ingredients not generally available this side of the 1200s.

THE PARIS POISONER

Catherine Deshayes Monvoisin, more commonly known as La Voisin, was a French sorceress, fortune teller and professional poisoner operating in the seventeenth century. She headed up a network of darkness, comprised of fortune tellers, alchemists and poisoners. She procured a variety of services for her clients – among them members of the aristocracy – including aphrodisiacs, abortion, magical services and poison, as well as arranging black masses.

La Voisin was a central figure in *l'affaire des poisons* (the affair of the poisons), which was a huge murder scandal in France in the 1670s during the reign of King Louis XIV. Her network of fiends is estimated to have led to the death of upward of 2,500 people and she is considered possibly the most successful serial murderer in history. Prominent members of French aristocracy were found to be involved in the scandal, and charged with counts of witchcraft and poisoning, with the eventual execution of 36 people.

La Voisin had turned to fortune telling when her husband went bankrupt and the family needed financial support. It turned out she was incredibly good at it – liked as she was by wealthy aristocrats and those close to the king – and the money kept rolling in. However, it wasn't long before she realized she could offer her clients more than fortunes and evolved her business to offer professional black magic. Clients seeking predictions about their future would often wish for things, such as for their desired to fall in love with them, their spouse to die so they might marry another or a relative to pass so they might inherit property or money. Somewhere along the path, La Voisin decided she could offer services to make these wishes come true.

For aphrodisiacs, she sold powders concocted from such ingredients as toad bones, mole teeth, human blood, iron filings and the dust of human remains. Should a client wish to bump someone off, La Voisin would procure a fatal poison from an apothecary belonging to her syndicate of undesirables.

The most famous of her clients was Madame de Montespan, mistress to the king. La Voisin supplied her with many a love potion to slip into the king's nightcap to quell her fears he would grow tired of her. However, when he did eventually become bored and dumped her, Montespan went to La Voisin with a new remit – this time she wanted to poison the king.

As luck – for the king's sake – would have it, around this time La Voisin's biggest business rival in the world of dark trade was arrested and threatened. She gave up La Voisin in an attempt to wriggle out of any charges for her own nefarious dealings, which led to the arrest of La Voisin and demise of her entire network of ne'er-do-wells.

The trial that followed became known as the affair of the poisons and the king demanded that everyone involved – including clients – were executed. He backtracked when the sheer number and prominence of the aristocrats in La Voisin's little black book became apparent. Even so, many members of high society were imprisoned or exiled as a result of the scandal.

La Voisin was executed publicly in 1680. Curiously, she was venerated by the public, who saw her as something of a saint, despite her many crimes.

SINISTER SKIN-WALKERS

The indigenous communities of North America have rich traditions and cultures, historically dipping their toes into the world of witchcraft with abandon.

In Navajo legend, witches tend to represent evil, thought to pervert the good work of healers, medicine men and women. Traditionally, healers learn about both good and dark magic to attain a thorough understanding of their work – but some become corrupt and choose the darkness over the light.

According to Navajo belief, when a witch – or skin-walker – travels in the darkness, they wear the skin of a dead animal in order to successfully transform into that creature. These shape-shifting abilities are alluded to in the Navajo saying *yee naaldlooshii*, meaning "with it, he goes on all fours".

Tending to assume the form of bears, wolves and coyotes, skin-walkers are considered to be extremely powerful and notoriously difficult to kill – they can only meet their end via a bullet or knife rubbed with white ash.

MASTER OF DARKNESS

Aleister Crowley is one of the most famous occultists in history, dividing opinion to this day – a sort of controversial love-him-or-loathe-him figure.

He wasn't just an occultist, but also a ceremonial magician, mountaineer, poet, novelist and painter. He had a penchant for a lot of drugs and sex and was branded an absolute genius by one camp and an evil, egotistical "traitor to the British people" by the other.

Born Edward Alexander Crowley to a wealthy, devoutly Christian family in 1875, he rebelled against his parents' religious values from a relatively young age and adopted the name Aleister at the age of 20. A couple of years later he joined the Hermetic Order of the Golden Dawn, a secret society dedicated to the practice and study of metaphysics, paranormal activity and the occult. Crowley became so devoted to the Order that he hired a senior member of the group to be his live-in tutor with whom he experimented with ceremonial magic and the ritualistic use of drugs.

He continued to pursue his non-black magic passions, accompanying a group of mountaineers in the first ever attempt to climb K2 and back in London rubbing shoulders with painter Gerald Kelly and sculptor Auguste Rodin.

In 1904, Crowley claimed to have heard the voice of the Egyptian god Horus attempting to communicate with him as he meditated. Believing Horus was sending him a message, Crowley set about writing *The Book of the Law*, which later became the cornerstone of Thelema, the religion he founded. He introduced his followers to the concept of "magick", using the new spelling to differentiate occult practices from performance magic.

In 1907, he founded the magical organisation A.A. Through a combination of ceremonial magic, yoga and essences of Buddhism, its members were dedicated to attaining a type of spiritual enlightenment through a series of initiations.

He continued to write furiously and published countless works on the occult. In 1920 he established the Abbey of Thelema in Sicily, where he and his followers experimented with drugs, sex and strange rituals. In 1923, one follower died shortly after a ritual in which he allegedly drank the blood of a cat. The Italian government were horrified and booted Crowley out of the country, after which the Abbey disbanded.

He continued to write and publish his occultist works for the next two decades, garnering fans and enemies in equal measure. He died in 1947 at the age of 72, his funeral – dubbed the "black mass" – was only attended by a very few people. A commentator at the time noted that although Crowley had become an infamous character and his intellect revered, he was not thought of fondly – however, those who knew him best said that he wouldn't have wanted to be.

In life he aroused in people anger, curiosity, horror, fear and loathing, and in death he continues to split opinion – this impressive and articulate man was as talented as he was nasty, and he used his intellect and dedication to learning to take himself and others to some incredibly dark places.

MAGIC VS MAGICK

We've all heard of "magic", but what about "magick"? Many people use the terms interchangeably, but there is an important difference. The dictionary suggests the latter to be an archaic spelling of the former and while that may be true, Aleister Crowley adopted "magick" to mean something a little different.

The more familiar "magic" is commonly understood to be a method of manipulating things or events by using mysterious or supernatural forces. However, "magick" was favoured by Crowley to differentiate his brand of it from the type of showmanship prone to pulling rabbits from hats. He also believed that "magick" described anything that could move someone to fulfil their destiny – their "True Will".

Crowley allegedly chose to add the "k" to the end of "magic" because, as the eleventh letter of the alphabet it had significance for him. It also meant he was dealing with a six-letter word, which tied in with the hexagrams that were prominent in his writings.

SLEEPLESS IN SALEM

Salem in Massachusetts is a small, historic city perched on the east coast of the USA. The harrowing witch trials of 1692–3 means that Salem will forever be associated with witchcraft and tragedy, its name still conjuring a certain darkness. The trials were more deeply inscribed on the paranormal consciousness when Arthur Miller used them as the basis for his much-revered play *The Crucible* (1953).

Visit today and you will be greeted with several gaudy museums and tourist experiences, detailing the story of the Salem witches and the actions that sealed their fate. Pose with the bronze statue of Elizabeth Montgomery of 1960s TV sitcom *Bewitched* fame and pause for reflection at the memorial dedicated to the fallen witches – a rare understated corner of this showy town. Visit on Halloween and prepare to have all of your senses assaulted.

The witch-hunt of the 1690s saw more than 200 people accused of practising witchcraft, referred to by the townspeople as "the Devil's magic", and the eventual execution of 20 Salem residents.

Three young local girls started behaving strangely – screaming, throwing, uttering peculiar sounds and contorting themselves – and it wasn't long before a doctor ruled the behaviour supernatural. The children were pressured by magistrates to explain who was responsible and pointed the finger at three local women, one – Tituba – was a slave working in the house of one of the children.

Two of the women denied all accusations of wrongdoing, but Tituba confessed that the Devil had come to her and insisted she serve him. She suggested there were other townsfolk practising the dark arts who were out to destroy the Puritans. All three women were jailed and, with paranoia riding high, many more were accused in the months that followed. One of the most controversial aspects of the trials was the fact that the court admitted spectral evidence to the proceedings. This allowed the use of testimony in which people claimed the accused had appeared to them in a dream or vision and done them harm in their imagination. The thinking at the time was that witches were able to project themselves in a spiritual fashion and cause harm from afar – able to physically manipulate their victims while being physically present elsewhere. Remote witchcraft, if you will. This spectral evidence led to the execution of 20 people – 19 of whom were hanged on Gallows Hill and one who was pressed to death with large stones.

By 1693, spectral evidence was banned from all trials in Salem and all who were in prison on charges of witchcraft were released, but the damage had been done. By 1697 many involved, including the judge responsible for overseeing proceedings, confessed their mistakes. By 1702 the trials had been deemed unlawful, and in 1711 pardons were issued and the families of those accused offered compensation. However, startlingly, it wasn't until 1957 that Massachusetts formally apologized for the injustice.

GRAVE INJUSTICE

In 1776, in the village of Doruchów in central Poland, a famous witch-hunt took place despite the abolition of sorcery investigations and witch trials in the country.

After the wife of a local aristocrat fell ill, the finger of blame was pointed at several women who lived in the village. Fourteen women were arrested and accused of causing the woman's sickness through the use of magic.

A trial took place, which saw the women grilled about their supposed supernatural influence over the noblewoman's health; three of the women were so badly tortured they died from their injuries and the remainder were burned at the stake.

The judges who oversaw the trial were punished for allowing it to take place despite magistrates having been banned from handling cases involving witchcraft. An all-out prohibition on witch trials, burning and torture was reinforced, but that wouldn't bring back the tortured and burned.

FANTASTICAL FAMILIARS

Sabrina has Salem, Mildred Hubble has Tabby, Dumbledore has Fawkes, Voldemort has Nagini and the Harry Potter-verse is divided as to whether Hedwig is a familiar or just a clever messenger. Witches have long been associated with their black-cat companions, with these relationships rooted in folklore and mythology. In Norse legend, the goddess Freja oversaw fertility, love, battle and death, as well as practising witchcraft and wielding a chariot pulled by magical cats.

These creatures are referred to as "familiars", "spirit guides" or "imps" and are purported to have supernatural powers, performing tasks for their black magic-practising owners. In seventeenth-century England, when witch fever was peaking and communities of women were being killed off for their supposed interest in magic – and plenty of them having never given it a second thought – a potential familiar was thought to be a sure sign of guilt.

Familiars were considered to be small, domestic creatures, such as cats – the obvious one – but also toads, dogs, birds, rats and moles, which many believed were the embodiment of the Devil. If you believed the rumours, their owners fed them lashings of their own blood, made them nests or allowed them to sleep in their bed with them. Many accused of witchcraft also admitted to meeting the Devil in the form of a black hound.

It was thought familiars also gave advice to their witches and taught them how to perform spells, while their humans used them as spies. These animals could also allegedly detect disease and ailments, which was above board and considered the work of good spirits. At one point in history, consulting a good spirit for help when a patient had a health issue that was stumping the medical professionals was actively encouraged.

There were reported confessions of people who claimed to have made a pact with their demonic familiar and instructed them to cause harm to those they had been wronged by. Some even believed black cats to be witches in disguise, and that familiars could also take a more human form – in the guise of fairies or ghosts.

Many, many dogs and cats were destroyed due to the paranoia at the time surrounding the dark arts, and some theories suggest this could have contributed to the spread of the plague – carried as it was by rodents that were no longer being caught by our feline and canine friends.

Philip Pullman's "daemons" in the *His Dark Materials* trilogy are a type of familiar that are the animalistic embodiment of a person's soul, their inner self. They are emotionally aware, intelligent and reflect their human's personality.

MARK OF THE WITCH

The "witch's mark" or "devil's mark", which was sought during investigations of witchcraft, was supposedly an indication of evil found on the skin of a purveyor of black magic, a permanent marking from the Devil himself signifying servitude and obedience to his diabolical ways.

People believed these marks took the form of scratch or claw marks across the skin, created by the Devil's hand, or scarred burn marks from a hot-iron branding. Warts, frequently associated with witches – one only need look at Disney for guidance – found anywhere on the body were thought to be teats, from where a witch would feed her familiar either milk or blood. There was also talk of the Devil dropping in on occasion to feed too.

Societal fear of bodily deformities and disabilities has been traced back to books, films, stories and folk tales in which villains – including witches – are often portrayed as having a physical abnormality that represents their marred soul and reinforces the character's "badness". This trope endured through history and is sadly still in force today in everything from Hollywood films to children's books.

During witchcraft trials around the seventeenth century, those suspected of witchcraft would find their bodies scrutinized for a mark of any kind. Anyone with a mole, wart, skin tag or insensitive patch of skin were in trouble. The accused were treated so horrendously that they would be stripped and shaved of all body hair in the search for a mark. The torturous practice of "pricking" was carried out whereby pins were driven into parts of a suspect's body, usually calluses and scars, in order to find an area where the victim had no feeling. If there were no marks at all on the body, pins were driven repeatedly into an accused witch's body until an area was deemed insensitive – and then they were brandished a true witch and put on trial. It was a tough old time in which to live.

PENDLE PERSECUTIONS

In the seventeenth century, Lancaster, in England's north-west, was a hotbed of suspected witchcraft, playing a major role in the witch trials and becoming one of the towns in which the trials were best documented.

The clerk of the court recorded the proceedings and documented them in an official publication, *The Wonderfull Discoverie of Witches in the Countie of Lancaster*, which was an unusual act, but became an incredibly important document in charting the history of witch persecution in England.

Lancaster was considered a darkened corner of England, supposedly wild and lawless, where residents did not respect the teachings of the church – instead remaining true to their Roman Catholic beliefs, despite Henry VIII's Reformation – and theft and violence were commonplace.

In the case of the Pendle witches, members of two rival families and others were put on trial for a number of crimes including the murder of up to ten people. The dead in question had perished years before but once the authorities had decided black magic was at play and pointed the finger at the suspects, they seemingly threw all their unsolved cases at them. The rival families accused each other of countless crimes, only adding fuel to the pyre.

 A total of 11 people – nine women and two men – were tried on counts of murder and the dark arts, ten of whom were found guilty and executed.

Modern-day Pendle memorializes the plight of its accused witches through various historical walking trails, sculptures dedicated to those who were hanged and experience tours, taking in every step of the story.

TALE OF A TALISMAN

A talisman – or amulet – is traditionally an object believed to have religious or magical powers that bring good luck to heal or protect their owner. Talismans can also ensure good health for and afford great power to – as well as harm – the individual for which they were made.

Talismans can be natural – think precious stones, metals, bones, plants, animal claws and teeth – or man-made, such as small figurines and medallions. They either derive their powers from natural forces or from their creation through ritual.

Ancient peoples including Neanderthals and Egyptians used talismans in burials, with some of the earliest figurines thought to date back to 25,000 BC. The ancient Egyptians favoured the use of talismans to represent different things – the most common being the scarab beetle, which represented life and carvings of which were worn in both life and death.

In the Middle Ages, the Christians used talismans in the form of relics of saints and supposed letters from Heaven, while in Islamic culture it is common to carry verses from the Qur'an or sacred numbers in a small satchel in order to keep them close and ensure their owner's safety.

Talismans have also been used in architecture in order to bestow good fortune on those living or working within a certain building.

HEALING PROWESS

Grigori Rasputin was a Russian mystic, rumoured to be a faith healer and to possess miraculous powers. He was a self-proclaimed holy man who declared he had the ability to predict the future and heal the sick.

In the early 1900s, intrigued by his supposed talents, the court circles of St Petersburg welcomed him in because they were experimenting with mysticism and the occult at the time. His prowess soon led to his introduction to Emperor Nicholas II and his wife Empress Consort Alexandra. Heir to the Russian Empire, their son Alexei suffered from haemophilia – the genetic disorder that impairs the ability for blood clots to form in the body – and they feared greatly for his life.

Believing Rasputin might be able to help, they called on him during one of their son's bleeding episodes and he was indeed able to cause the blood to clot. Many sceptics believed the only rational explanation at the time was hypnosis. As Rasputin left the palace that day, he told the Emperor that the future of both their child and their empire lay in his hands.

From that day forth Rasputin became a valued member of the royal family's entourage, with the worried parents believing he could heal their son's condition, as well as bring good fortune or recognize omens concerning the future of the Russian Empire.

Rasputin continued to purportedly "heal" Alexei, allegedly bringing him back from death's door in 1912, in what many considered to be his performance of "a miracle", with doctors who had examined Alexei claiming the recovery to be "wholly inexplicable from a medical point of view".

Despite his good behaviour and healing potential around the palace, out in the real world Rasputin was a menace, his behaviour apparently scandalous and often reported to the tsar. He was initially banished, but Alexandra insisted he was of vital importance in matters pertaining to Alexei's health and so Rasputin was reinstated in his role as holy man and healer at the palace.

By 1915, with the First World War in full swing, Rasputin was so trusted by the Russian royal family that he had profound influence at the palace in matters ranging from battle tactics to the appointment of church officials and cabinet ministers. His decisions were generally disastrous and he had to fend off numerous assassination attempts from Russians who claimed to have the empire's best interests at heart.

In December 1916, though, he was successfully assassinated, although it was no simple affair. After being poisoned, which did not succeed, he was shot, but was able to run away, and finally was thrown into a river through a hole in the ice. Mere weeks later the Russian Revolution began, signalling the rise of international communism and the formation of the Soviet Union.

MYTHICAL CREATURES

The world is awash with stories of creatures we know little about – and this only adds to the intrigue. Do you think people would be so interested if the Loch Ness Monster had been caught 50 years ago and you could visit it in a zoo? If it had been poked and prodded by every eminent biologist in the world, and they had all answered every question and offered their theories about how it came into being?

Famous cases of cryptids such as Bigfoot and Nessie produce such a plethora of reported sightings and command such a legion of fans that they have their own official organisations in order to keep track of activity and notify everyone. I imagine there's a membership badge in it for you, if you're interested.

From the big-hitters to the little known, we'll travel the world on a wave of cryptozoology, taking in ice men, jackalopes, mothmen, demon goats, giant lizards, swamp monsters, a Minotaur, fairies, sea beasts – and let's not forget Gef, the talking mongoose.

BEWARE THE BIGFOOT

If you spend long enough and look hard enough in the thick of the forest of Washington state in the USA, you might just catch sight of the notorious Bigfoot. Also known as the Sasquatch, this hairy, tall creature resembles a giant ape that walks upright, strides like a human and is thought to predominantly inhabit this corner of the USA, with sightings spilling over the border into Canada.

Bigfoot has been spotted all over the country, in Ohio, Georgia, Florida, California and even New Jersey, but the Pacific Northwest is a veritable hotspot and the stretch of land from Washington to Oregon is regarded as the creature's stomping ground.

Hundreds of sightings are reported every year and, excited or terrified, witnesses log their encounters with the Bigfoot Field Researchers Organization, which keeps track of the hairy giant's activity across the country as well as continually investigating evidence for the creature's existence and organizing expeditions across the country to track it down.

Standing on two feet, the Sasquatch is thought to be between 1.8 m (6 ft) and 4.6 m (15 ft tall), gives off a foul odour and will either move stealthily or emit a high-pitched howl. Bigfoot was so named for the enormous footprints it leaves behind, of which there are also hundreds upon hundreds of reports every year. The prints have measured up to 60 cm (24 in.) in length and 20 cm (8 in.) in width – far larger than any documented creature in these parts.

Residents of the Pacific Northwest have become accustomed to stumbling upon these giant footprints while out on a hike, finding clumps of thick fur caught in branches or smelling strange odours in the forest, and it's not unusual to hear locals speak of a tall and imposing figure between the trees watching them from afar.

One terrifying story from the 1920s saw a group of miners recount how they were attacked by several tall, hairy "ape men". They took shelter in a cabin, only for the creatures to hurl rocks at the building and slam their bodies into the walls. Another report from around the same time is of a man who claimed he was abducted by a creature matching the Sasquatch's description and held captive by its family for a week. He asserted that the Bigfoot family did not cause him any harm but instead were amused by him.

While the creature remains elusive enough to have evaded capture over the years – folklore says that the Sasquatch spends most of its time sleeping and protecting its young – it has been captured on film a few times. Footage is often considered controversial or dismissed as a hoax due to the unfortunate fact that Bigfoot looks rather like a taller-than-average man in a hairy suit.

The Sasquatch crossed into the world of UFOs in the 1970s, when a woman allegedly saw one board a flying saucer outside her home in Cincinnati, USA. Many cryptozoologists are open to the idea that cryptids hail from another world and were either abandoned here on Earth or are the product of alien experiments.

MONGOLIAN DEATH WORM MYSTERY

Deep in the Gobi desert of Mongolia, many believe a huge, deadly worm-like creature exists hidden beneath the desert sands.

The worm is said to be a metre long, dark red and with spikes at each end. Locals call it Olgoi-khorkhoi, which loosely translates as "large intestine worm" and over the centuries they have supposedly been spotted by numerous people passing through the desert. The worm purportedly spends most of its time beneath the sand, but if one is ever seen on the surface it is given a wide berth.

The worm apparently has the capacity to inflict death in various ways – including launching a stream of corrosive, lethal venom or electrocuting victims from a distance.

The worm has never been photographed but has appeared in numerous writings and many believe these narratives are rooted in historical fact. A number of trips have been made to unearth the death worm, but none have succeeded – and yet still people seek the truth about this terrifying creature straight out of a 1950s comic book.

THE DEVIL LIVES IN JERSEY

On the east coast of America, in small-town New Jersey around the Pinelands, resides the local myth of the Jersey Devil. This creature is described as having a body similar to that of a kangaroo, with a goat's head and leathery, bat-like wings. With cloven hooves, clawed hands and a forked tail, you can see how it came to be named "Devil", and its swift, darting movements and blood-curdling screams only add terror to the image.

It is said that in the early 1700s a woman with 12 children found she was pregnant for the thirteenth time and cursed the unborn child as "the devil" in a fit of frustration. The child was born in human form, but quickly transformed into the winged, goat-headed, cloven-hooved creature, then growled and screeched and disappeared up the chimney.

Over the centuries there have been numerous sightings of the Jersey Devil. It has been blamed for several livestock killings, and mysterious animal tracks have been discovered and screams heard. In 1909 there was a spike in encounters with the creature, with almost 1,000 reports flooding in. In the 1920s a farmer shot a creature that was attempting to steal his chickens. He photographed the dead beast and showed the image to more than 100 people, with none able to identify it. Many believe it was the Jersey Devil – or one of them. Around the same time a cab driver claimed a large-winged creature attacked his vehicle, pounding on the roof as he changed a tyre.

In the late 1950s and early 60s there were several sightings and a whopping $250,000 reward was offered for the live capture of the Jersey Devil, with plans to house it in its own private zoo. Needless to say, it was never captured.

Reports have been sparser lately, with the odd sighting in the 1970s, 80s and 90s. However, in 2015, a man was driving when he saw what he thought was a black llama in the middle of the road, but he claimed the figure then spread its wings and flew up into the sky. Of course, he captured it on video using his smartphone and the footage went viral. Take a look and decide for yourself.

A TROLL FOL-DE-ROL

In the lush, green expanse of the Yorkshire Dales, amid hills, rocks, caves and crags, lurks many a tale of the monsters that once resided here.

Along with impish beings thought to live in these rural areas, were more malicious ones – among them the troll. Trolls were nocturnal and lived in caves, of which there is a vast underground network in these parts of England. If they found themselves out in the open when day broke, they would turn to stone where they stood.

Trolls had a big head, green eyes and stumpy legs, with feet like a bird, and were known to steal children and lure people to their deaths.

Trollers Gill, a limestone gorge near the village of Appletreewick in North Yorkshire, is thought to be so named for its associated history with these creatures. One story tells of a local farmer travelling on a nearby road taking his fresh goods to market, when he heard a cry for help. He drove his horse and cart toward Trollers Gill and fell into the chasm. Many believed the trolls had lured him there and urged him to jump over the gorge.

Along with the trolls, Trollers Gill is thought to be haunted by a spectral hound, reported to be as big as a small horse, black and shaggy, with "eyes as big as saucers".

LIZARD MAN RAMPAGE

Around the swamps of Bishopville in South Carolina, USA, locals say a terrifying creature emerges at night at the height of summer and attacks cars in the local area.

In June 1988, late one night a teenage boy was driving home along the edge of Scape Ore swamp when his tyre went flat. Luckily, he had a spare, so he got out of the car to change it. Suddenly he heard someone running toward him and out of the darkness he saw what he could only describe as a lizard man – standing 2 m (7 ft) tall, with red eyes, green scaly skin, and three fingers with long black claws. Terrified, the boy jumped back into his car and locked the doors. The lizard man proceeded to attack the car, ripping off the wing mirrors, and banging and chewing the roof.

Two weeks later, a car was vandalized close to the same spot – there were deep scratches along the sides, the fenders had been ripped off and the chrome trim looked like it had been chewed. As summer rolled on, close to the swamp more and more car owners woke up to find their cars had been scratched and chewed in the night. The police were always called and on one occasion they made a plaster cast of a huge three-toed footprint in the mud.

As the weather cooled off, so the car vandalism subsided, and although there have been sightings and car attacks since then, they have been few and far between. In 2015, a woman claimed to have photographic evidence of the lizard man, however she produced a crystal-clear photograph of what could only be described as a person in a lizard costume – whether she was aware of this or not no one is quite sure.

Local news took this seriously, however, even if the rest of the world wasn't so sure, with reports warning the public to be on their guard. In 2017, further news coverage urged locals to be vigilant as the solar eclipse approached – in case this nocturnal beast mistook a total solar eclipse for the onset of nightfall.

As with so many of these cases, there are two camps – the sceptics and the believers. Nevertheless, the car attacks seen through the summer of 1988 and afterward remain a mystery to many – clearly the work of a huge animal, is the lizard man to blame?

APEMAN OF THE MOUNTAINS

It is believed by some that deep in the mountains of Pakistan lives a creature the locals call the Barmanou. This being supposedly possesses human and ape-like characteristics and eyewitnesses have described it as a living Neanderthal. The Barmanou is known for abducting women and attempting to mate with them.

Shepherds living in the mountains have recounted seeing the creatures often, with one declaring they have seen a mother and child holding hands. Extensive searches for the Barmanou in the late 1980s led to the amassing of many first-hand accounts, while in the 1990s during a hunt in the Shishi Kuh valley scientists reported hearing unusual guttural sounds that they deduced could only have been produced by a primate.

Often referred to as Pakistan's equivalent of Bigfoot or the Yeti, the Barmanou is said to be 1.8 m (6 ft) tall, wears animal skins on its back and head, and is said to only come down into the valley during periods of heavy snowfall.

LOCH NESS MYSTERY

The idea of a Loch Ness Monster was popularized in Scotland in the 1930s when an initial sighting led to another, and then another, and a famous photograph materialized of a diplodocus-like creature with a long neck protruding from the dark waters. Locals had always touted the story of a leviathan in the loch but this was when the sightings truly began. For 60 years the photograph was considered evidence for the existence of a creature beneath the surface of Loch Ness, until in 1994 after much research and scrutiny it was deemed an elaborate hoax.

However, reports of an unusual creature in the area date back as far as the sixth century, where claims of a "water beast" attacking swimmers in the nearby River Ness have been found in published writings from the era. Evidence of further sightings after this are few and far between, until the 1930s when Nessie-mania set in.

An article in the *Inverness Courier* in 1933 described the sighting of an enormous "whale-like fish" churning in the water of the Loch. Later that year a couple driving by the Loch claimed the monster crossed the road in front of them, alleging it to be "a most extraordinary form of animal", around 1.2 m (4 ft) tall and 8 m (25 ft) long, with a long and thin wavy neck.

MYTHICAL CREATURES

Over the years various expeditions have set out to hunt down the monster, but to no avail, and in the 1950s sonar readings taken by a fishing boat found a large object was keeping pace with the vessel at a depth of 146 m (479 ft). The boat tracked the object for around 800 m (2,600 ft) before it lost contact.

In 1987, Operation Deepscan tasked a fleet of 24 boats equipped with high-tech equipment with conducting a thorough search of the loch. They made sonar contact with an object of unusually large size and detected movement. One sonar expert involved in the operation reported there was something in the loch larger than a fish and that perhaps it was "some species that hasn't been detected before".

Alleged video footage and photographs of the monster have appeared sporadically since the 1930s – with people even claiming to have spotted Nessie on Google Earth – but many remain sceptical. There are plenty of believers out there though, so why not take a trip to Loch Ness to find out for yourself?

MINNESOTA ICEMAN

In the 1960s and 70s a sideshow exhibit of a human-like ape creature frozen in a block of ice toured North America, appearing at carnivals, state fairs and in shopping malls. The "iceman" claimed to provide the missing link between man and Neanderthal, was 1.8 m (6 ft) in height, covered in hair, with very large hands and feet. Its arm was broken and it only had one eye, due to its death via a bullet entering the back of its head.

The exhibitor of the iceman claimed it had been discovered in Siberia, Russia, and that he had been charged with taking care of it for its rich and eccentric owner. The caretaker of the creature was once detained at the Canadian border, when officials were concerned he was transporting a human body and on a separate occasion a concerned citizen reported him to the FBI, worried the iceman might in fact be a murder victim.

The FBI, along with others, suspected the iceman was a hoax, fabricated from latex and hair, and did not pursue an investigation. However, there will always be true believers and in 2013 the iceman himself was sold on eBay for $20,000 to the Museum of the Weird in Austin, Texas.

BEAST ON THE MOOR

Stories of the so-called Beast of Bodmin Moor have intrigued and baffled many for decades. Bodmin Moor in north Cornwall in the UK is a remote, bleak, heather-clad landscape, scattered with granite rocks and grazed on by wild ponies.

The "beast" locals speak of is a black cat the size of a puma that allegedly stalks the moor and since 1978 has been sighted by as many as 60 people. Eyewitnesses describe a large, dark, feline creature with yellow eyes and big, sharp teeth. A string of incidents involving mysteriously mutilated livestock have been blamed on the beast and people have reported being chased by it, frightened by its powerful nature. Many have spotted it from afar, still and watching, and there are many photographs that supposedly depict the creature – however, with few people willing to get too close the quality isn't always that great.

Theories surrounding the mysterious inhabitant of Bodmin Moor are plenty, but the most plausible explanations point to actual pumas. Rumours of a zoo in nearby Plymouth releasing three pumas into the wild following the closure of the facility in the 1970s would appear to fit the story nicely. Others believe the beast is an illegal pet, either released or escaped and never reported due to its unofficial status. These stories would explain the sighting of the beast in the 1970s and 80s, perhaps even the 90s, but what about those closer to the present day?

Some theories suppose that the pumas may have found similar creatures to mate with and continued the beastly line, while others prefer to think that it is a species of antisocial British wild cat thought to be long extinct living quietly on the edges of the moor. As you would expect, those of a paranormal proclivity like to stick with the idea the beast is a ghostly echo of a creature that wandered the moors of Cornwall in days of yore.

In the 1990s a boy found a large cat's skull measuring 10 cm (4 in.) by 18 cm (7 in.) in a nearby river, which only provoked Bodmin beast enthusiasts to proclaim that those grainy images pointed to the truth. However, the skull was found to have been imported as part of a leopard-skin rug, as it contained tropical cockroach egg casings. And in 1995 the UK government carried out an official investigation into the potential existence of a beast on the moor, but found no evidence of a big cat resident.

DEMONIC GOATS

In 2017, in a remote Indian village, a goat was born with a head and features that looked remarkably like a human's. Photographs were posted on social media and immediately went viral – the villagers were terrified and the online community disturbed.

With its smooth skin devoid of fur and oddly human features (its face shape, spacing of its eyes, a nose that bent inward, and protruding lips and chin) locals assumed the goat to be some kind of demon.

A goat born earlier that same summer in Argentina had a similarly demonic face, with bulging eyes and a flat visage. Despite the beast being stillborn, locals of the San Luis province were alarmed and frightened at what its arrival could mean.

Experts have pointed to the likelihood of these goats being the product of genetic mutations, however that doesn't stop the conspiracy theorists from suggesting the biologically impossible idea that a human bred with a goat, or that the creatures were messages sent from the underworld in a demonic version of UPS.

IS IT A MOTH? IS IT A MAN?

Since first being documented in the 1960s in Point Pleasant, West Virginia, the Mothman has become one of America's most talked-about mythical creatures. He has been sighted countless times flying through the air, often jumping from one tree to another, and many believe him to be a harbinger of cataclysmic events.

In November 1966, in a town close to Point Pleasant, a group of men were digging a grave when a shadowy figure flew over their heads. Later that week two young couples travelling together in a car nearby claimed they were chased by a dark figure with glowing red eyes and a 3 m (10 ft) wingspan. Over the following year there were multiple sightings of this creature – later dubbed "Mothman" by an Ohio newspaper.

Locals theorized the creature was a product of a government experiment, perhaps nuclear weapons testing, and that it lived in a former, now-vacant power plant on the edge of town. The area had supposedly once been home to a classified government facility, so in the realms of paranormal explanations it's all pretty plausible.

In December 1967, just over a year since the first sighting, the Silver Bridge connecting Point Pleasant to Ohio collapsed during rush hour and tumbled into the Ohio River below.

Tragically 46 people died and two bodies were never recovered. After the catastrophe the Mothman sightings ceased, leading conspiracy theorists to assert the two were linked because the creature was a signifier of impending doom and that instances of locals glimpsing him were in fact premonitions of the bridge collapse.

The Mothman seeped into popular culture with the publication of John Keel's 1975 book *The Mothman Prophecies*, which linked the sightings with the bridge tragedy. The book was given the Hollywood treatment and a film adaptation starring Richard Gere and Laura Linney was released in 2002.

Following the Mothman's entrance into the mainstream, there were further sightings in West Virginia and elsewhere across the USA. Point Pleasant enjoyed the interest directed at the town and capitalized on it heartily with an annual Mothman Festival that draws as many as 12,000 enthusiasts each year – as well as erecting a fierce-looking 3.7 m (12 ft) Mothman statue in the town, its bejewelled red eyes glinting in the sun on a bright day. Visitors to this corner of West Virginia can also absorb an extensive and detailed history of the creature at the Mothman museum and buy a T-shirt in a variety of colours, before heading to the Mothman Urban Legends Bar & Grill for "Chupacabra chicken wings", "Jersey Devil deep fried mushrooms" and "Kraken crab cakes". What are you waiting for?

JEWEL THIEVES BEWARE

Among the caves of the Richtersveld of South Africa or in the Orange River of the North Eastern Cape province, there purportedly lives an enormous, "elephant-sized" serpent. Its scales are black as night and it is thought to be 6–12 m (20–40 ft) long.

The Grootslang dwells in a cave known as the Bottomless Pit, which connects to the sea many miles away. The story goes that the cave is filled with diamonds – a classic lure for jewel-hungry humans from a human-hungry beast.

Its neck and tail take the form of a snake, while its body is bulky like an elephant. According to fable the Grootslang was created by the gods, though deemed to be too strong and cunning. The gods supposedly decided to create two animals from the Grootslang – the first elephants and snakes – however one beast escaped the gods.

In 1917 a British businessman vanished while searching for treasure in the Richtersveld – as you can imagine, all blame fell on the Grootslang and this renewed the sense of terror among locals about the network of caves.

HOLD ON TO YOUR LIVESTOCK

First reported in Puerto Rico in 1995, the chupacabra is said to be a monster that attacks livestock and drains their blood. Translating as "goat-sucker" the chupacabra apparently does not discriminate when it comes to dinner, also targeting chickens, rabbits, sheep, cats and dogs. Hundreds of farm animals in Puerto Rico were being discovered with all their blood sucked out of them and no one knew why.

That was until 1995, when a woman spotted an "alien-like" creature outside her home in Canóvanas, east of San Juan. She described the chupacabra as a bipedal being with reptilian scales, black eyes and spines bristling along its back, adding that it hopped like a kangaroo and had an odour much like sulphur. Subsequent sightings were of a creature walking on four legs with the addition of a tail.

As word of the chupacabra and the dead farm animals travelled across to Central, South and North America, other countries began speaking out about their animals dying under similar circumstances. Farmers in Mexico, Colombia, Argentina, Chile and the USA all complained of unexplained grisly livestock deaths and wanted to know more about this mysterious bloodsucking monster.

More dog-like descriptions of a supposed chupacabra were offered up by further eyewitnesses and people began to theorize that these beasts could in fact be hairless dogs, coyotes or other canine relatives. Starting in the 2000s in the south-western states of the USA, around a dozen creatures matching the chupacabra's description have been found dead, described as being hairless, with four legs and what resembles burned skin.

Experts cite sarcoptic mange – a nasty and very contagious skin disease that causes fur to fall out, skin to thicken and unpleasant scabs to develop – as a possible explanation for the misidentification of a bloodsucking beast.

The thick skin and scabs might account for the supposed scales, and the patchy fur might be misinterpreted as spines across the back, but what of the bloodsucking until death?

Exsanguination is just not associated with dog-like animals and Puerto Rican farmers are quick to assert that their livestock have never been attacked by canines in the past.

References to the chupacabra have seeped into popular culture and there is even an *X-Files* episode dedicated to the creature. Despite the dog theories, many still believe there is a bloodsucking beast out there and have yet to be convinced otherwise.

DEEP-RED COLOSSUS

Deep in the waters of Uchiura Bay in Hokkaido, Japan, lurks a gigantic creature that is half-human and half-octopus, so they say. The Akkorokamui is supposedly a whopping 120 m (390 ft) long, its body can stretch to cover 10,000 sq m (1 hectare) and is a striking red colour, likened to the shade of the water as the sun sets.

This tentacled beast is so huge it can swallow whales and ships whole, and its colossal size causes the sky and sea to turn red when it emerges from the water. For centuries sailors and fishing boats have heeded the warning of a red sea and sky – and stayed well away.

The creature's origins are rooted in Shintoism and it is revered in some cultures as a deity, with its ability to self-amputate and regrow limbs affording it a sacred reputation for healing powers. Followers believe giving offerings to the Akkorokamui will help to heal their ailments, particularly disfigurement and broken limbs.

CHAOS AT CHRISTMAS

Alpine folklore tells of a Santa's helper of sorts who hones in on the naughty kids in and around Austria. Said to be half-goat, half-demon, Krampus has horns, hooves and a forked tail, and is a seriously frightening prospect for children. The good cop to St Nicholas's bad cop, Krampus is said to arrive alongside St Nick on December 5 – *Krampusnacht* (Krampus Night) – wearing a creepy wooden mask, animal skins and bells so you can hear him coming. While St Nick leaves gifts, his demon helper will apparently beat misbehaving children with a branch. In more extreme versions of the story, Krampus will eat the children or capture them in a basket and take them to hell. Absolutely. Terrifying. How do these children sleep at night? Or are Austrian infants the best behaved in the world?

According to the fable, Krampus is the son of Hel, god of the underworld in Norse mythology and the Austrian traditions are thought to be rooted in pre-Christian, pagan culture. The historic traditions are heartily upheld in many an Alpine town and the *Krampuslauf* (Krampus Run) sees hordes of people dressed as the frightening creature parading through the streets, doing their damned best to scare spectators silly, often chasing them and occasionally entering people's houses. It is apparently customary to offer the Krampuses schnapps, and it has to be said their masks and costumes only seem to grow more elaborate and horrifying each year.

While the celebrations in big towns and cities are more orderly and formal, with dedicated organisations taking charge and preparing throughout the year, it's a different story in the smaller towns where chaos can still reign. It can be a chaotic affair with sinister undertones, and it's been suggested its expanding popularity is a response to the over-commercialization of Christmas.

Krampus has entered popular culture in the rest of the world more recently thanks to horror films, books, and references in well-loved TV shows and video games.

JUNGLE FAMILY

According to Malaysian legend, deep in the jungle of Johor resides a 3 m (10 ft) tall, bipedal, black-fur-clad beast known as the Orang Mawas. The creature, which has allegedly been spotted raiding orchards and feeding on fish, is referred to as *hantu jarang gigi* by locals, which translates as "snaggle-toothed ghost".

Sightings have been recorded as far back as 1871 and some believe the Orang Mawas is a descendant of a long-extinct ape from the Middle Pleistocene age some 770,000–126,000 years ago.

In the 1990s large tracks with four toes were discovered and attributed to the creature, while in 2005 a much-reported sighting occurred. Three workers digging a pond spotted a family of two adults and a child near the Kincin River. Their incredible experience was backed up when enormous humanoid footprints were discovered – one 46 cm (18 in) in length.

Photographs of the footprints were published in a Malaysian newspaper, and the authorities launched an official investigation and subsequent investigation into the existence of the Orang Mawas. In 2006 a news story claimed one of the creatures had been captured, but this later turned out to be a hoax. And so the search continues.

JUMPING JACKALOPES

The jackalope is a well-known mythical creature, particularly across North America. With "jackalope" itself a portmanteau of "jackrabbit" and "antelope", if you haven't heard of this creature before you will no doubt be able to gather what it looks like.

North American folklore places the jackalope in the "fearsome critters" category, along with the cactus cat (a feline creature with hair-like thorns), gumberoo (a hairless bear with impenetrable skin), teakettler (a mouse-like creature that makes a noise like a kettle) and squonk (a sad animal with a tendency to literally dissolve into tears). Fearsome critters were the stuff of tall tales originating in the Great Lakes region of the USA and Canada, said to inhabit the sparsely populated land around the logging camps.

According to legend, a jackalope can imitate the human voice and cowboys from the days of the Old West would apparently insist they could hear the creatures impersonating them as they sat around the campfire. Its favourite tipple is whisky, so this is obviously how you would entice it; it is very agile, able to perform impressive backflips and dodge predators incredibly effectively; and it understands human language.

In the 1930s two hunter brothers with tendencies for taxidermy attached a set of antlers to the head of a deceased jackrabbit they had caught and sold it to a hotel in Douglas, Wyoming. Getting wind of this extraordinary mounted creature, other hotels, businesses and regular people wanted a piece of this antlered furry being, so the brothers set up a production line and created more jackalopes in order to cater to demand.

Fast-forward to the present day and the jackalope is well and truly rooted in popular culture, appearing in myriad children's books, songs, company logos, films and TV shows. Sports teams have been named after the creature (see Texas's now defunct Odessa Jackalopes) and craft beers brewed under its aegis (see Nashville's Jackalope Brewing Company, joyously founded by women in an incredibly male-dominated industry). Taxidermists still create mounted jackalopes, which can be found on many a bar-room wall up and down the USA, and the creature has been commercialized somewhat with statues and tourist tat aplenty.

Despite its history as a very obviously, although still much-loved, dreamt-up and then manufactured legendary creature, some still insist it to be real. Many still travel to Wyoming specifically to hunt and attempt to trap a jackalope in order to prove its existence. However, experts believe sightings of horned hares could be explained as rabbits suffering from a virus that causes antler- or horn-like tumours to sprout out of its head and body.

SWAMP SASQUATCH

Sometimes referred to as the Cajun Sasquatch, the Honey Island Swamp Monster is reported to live in the swamp in St Tammany Parish, Louisiana, USA. Ape-like in appearance and covered in silvery grey hair, it is said to be a towering 2 m (7 ft) tall, with yellow or red eyes, and is often accompanied by an unpleasant smell.

Sightings date back to the 1960s and Super 8 film footage supposedly shows the creature out and about on the bayou. Unusually large, four-toed footprints have been found and plaster casts taken, only adding to the evidence pot.

Some believe a train crash in the area in which a travelling circus lost its chimpanzees is an explanation for the sightings of the ape-like creature, the animals accepting the swamps as their new home and adapting to the environment accordingly.

Many tour companies in the area like to use the legend of the swamp monster to their advantage and will tell tales about the creature that lives on in local lore. Is this perhaps a desperate bid to have a slice of the Bigfoot publicity pie down in the bayous of Louisiana?

SERENADING SIRENS

Think of mermaids and depending on your persuasion your first thoughts might be of Disney's Ariel from *The Little Mermaid*, or perhaps Hans Christian Andersen's tale upon which that animated classic is based and the popular statue that sits by the waterside in Copenhagen to honour the Danish author and his creation.

Thought to sing sweetly yet hauntingly in order to lure sailors and their ships toward rocks and ultimately shipwreck, mermaids go back a long way. The sirens of Greek mythology were depicted as half-bird and half-woman, before evolving to the half-fish, half-woman version we are familiar with today – and the first-known stories of the aquatic creatures originate in Assyria in 1000 BC. Mythos has it that the goddess Atargatis was in love with a mortal, accidentally killed him and in her anguish – and perhaps to evade culpability – jumped into a lake and became a fish. Unfortunately, her divine beauty could not be concealed by the waters, so she morphed into a mermaid – only taking human form above the waist.

Legends popularized in the Middle East bespeak sea people, anatomically identical to humans but with the ability to breathe and live underwater, and breed with land-dwelling humans. While European folklore features a mermaid-like being with two fish tails. Alexander the Great's sister allegedly attained eternal life and after her death turned into a mermaid and went to live in the Aegean Sea. Supposedly she would ask sailors on passing ships of the health of King Alexander and, reassured on hearing he was well, would calm stormy waters and allow their ships to pass safely.

In Cornish folklore the Mermaid of Zennor was a beautiful woman who would attend the local church and sing more sweetly and serenely than anyone else in the congregation. She attended church infrequently over a period of many years but never seemed to age and no one knew anything about her. She took an interest in a young man with a beautiful voice, who after following her home was never seen again. She was not seen again either until a mermaid bearing her resemblance appeared to a sailor in a nearby cove and asked him to raise his anchor as it was resting on the door to her home and her children were inside. The sailor did as he was told and took the story back to the parish.

Sightings over the centuries have been too numerous to list, but a few worthy of note include Christopher Columbus claiming to have spotted three mermaids off the coast of Hispaniola and declaring them to not be as beautiful as they were represented; Blackbeard writing in his logbook that his crew should stay away from enchanted waters inhabited by merfolk and mermaids; and a crowd of people in Haifa Bay, Israel, claiming to have witnessed a mermaid leaping out of the water and performing somersaults – which led to a $1 million reward being offered for proof of its existence.

There have also been numerous and elaborate mummified and preserved mermaid specimens (supposedly), most of which have been proclaimed hoaxes – and none, it must be said were in any way aesthetically pleasing as the legends suggest – but the odd one has baffled researchers, as even after DNA testing its species could not be determined.

HAIR-RAISING ENCOUNTER

Venezuelan hairy dwarves are like smaller, super-smart versions of Bigfoot. Shorter than the average human at around 90 cm (3 ft) tall, these creatures are covered in long, bristly fur, their eyes glow green and they can be quite ferocious.

Most interestingly, they are believed to be technologically adept (I'm thinking Station from Bill and Ted – is anyone with me?) and are often associated with early UFO sightings. When the first glimpses of UFOs were reported, inhabitants of spacecrafts were often described as being short and hairy, rather than the "Take me to your leader" alien that has been popularized over the past half a century.

In the 1950s, two men on a hunting trip up the Amazon in Venezuela claim to have seen four hairy dwarf-like creatures dismounting a hovering spacecraft and attempting to abduct another two men out hunting. One of the men allegedly struck a dwarf with the butt of his rifle only to find it shattered on impact.

FOOTPRINTS IN THE SNOW

Deep in the Himalayas in Nepal, lives the beast, the legend, the Abominable Snowman. Now here's a cryptid that's a definite household name, so entrenched in modern popular culture I dare you to deny ever having come across it – it even has a ride dedicated to its supposed existence at Disneyland (Expedition Everest, in case you're wondering).

The Abominable Snowman is the Western name for the Yeti, whose origins are traced back through Sherpa folklore to the Asian Himalayas. It is described as a huge, muscular, ape-like creature, with grey or white fur and big, sharp teeth – like a snowy Bigfoot. Sometimes referred to as a dangerous "wild man", this elusive creature has been spotted over the years, but most photographic and video evidence remains grainy and hard to decipher. While it has left tracks in the snow, of which photographs have been taken, many believe it lives below the snow line.

The Yeti is supposed to have origins in the ancient beliefs of the Himalayans, where a group of people worshipped a so-called "glacier being" god of the hunt, depicted as an ape-like beast that carries a large stone for protection and use as a weapon. Apparently, Alexander the Great demanded to see a Yeti upon conquering this part of the world but was fobbed off with a line about the creatures not being able to come down from the mountains as they could not survive at a low altitude.

In 1921, the term "Abominable Snowman" was coined when a journalist interviewed a group of British explorers fresh from an expedition to Mount Everest. They claimed to have found large footprints that their guide attributed to what loosely translated as "man-bear snow-man". The journalist botched the translation to "filthy snowman" which didn't make the most appealing of headlines, so he adapted it to sound far more ferocious and frightening than the guide's original description.

In the 1940s hikers described seeing two ape-like creatures some distance below them on the mountain. They described them as 2.4 m (8 ft) in height, with a square head, sloped shoulders and a powerful chest; while another sighting around that time was of a beast emitting a high-pitched cry while it grubbed up roots from the mountainside.

In 1960, Sir Edmund Hillary, the first man to climb Everest (along with the under-mentioned Tenzing Norgay) said he had found a scalp belonging to a Yeti, which was later deemed by experts to belong to a goat-like creature; and a finger preserved and displayed in a monastery in Nepal that long claimed it belonged to a Yeti caused ripples throughout the Bigfoot and Yeti fan community for many years. However, upon examination in 2011 researchers found the finger actually belonged to a human, possibly an old monk who had died at the monastery.

In 2013 an extensive research project was carried out by Oxford University in an attempt to get to the bottom of the Yeti myth. Collectors and believers from around the world were asked to send samples of what they believed to be the big hairy one's teeth, hair or tissue collected at sightings.

It was discovered that most of the samples matched up on the DNA database with well-known animals. However, two of the samples fit with a species that lived anything up to 120,000 years ago – a suspected hybrid of a polar bear and a brown bear.

Could this be the answer Yeti believers have been looking for? A rare and elusive creature from a distant age that lives on in the Nepalese mountain wilderness? Perhaps...

ENCHANTING ENCANTADO

Friends of fishermen along the Amazon, the Encantado – meaning "enchanted one" – are a legendary part-human, part-dolphin creature said to come to the rescue of those in distress.

Thought to have some say in the weather, wielding a certain power over violent storms and guiding boats to safety, the pink aquatic organisms are also known for coming to the aid of humans at risk from drowning in the water.

Legend has it that each year at various Brazilian festival celebrations, the Encantado shape-shifts from its dolphin state into a young and handsome man dressed all in white and wearing a hat to cover the unchanged blowhole and conceal his true identity.

The man-version of the Encantado during festival season is far more sinister than its fishermen-friendly incarnation, supposedly attending celebratory events in order to woo, kidnap and impregnate young women. Women are apparently told that if they meet a handsome stranger at a festival he will likely be an Encantado. Perhaps nothing more than a ruse delivered by parents to keep young women away from strange men? Would you buy it?

DO YOU BELIEVE IN FAIRIES?

In more modern times, the thought of a fairy might conjure images of pink taffeta and flammable fancy-dress wings, or Disney-style beings waving magic wands and granting wishes.

However, the history of fairies goes back a long way. Rooted in Greek mythology are the fairy-like dryads and nymphs – spirits of the trees and rivers – and paganism venerated these creatures as gods, worshipping nature and all that had a hand in it.

In some circles fairies are kind and helpful, setting travellers back on the right path, while in others they are liable to trick humans, steal food and attack their homes. Centuries ago people believed they stole human babies and replaced them with their own, or kidnapped new mothers and forced them to breastfeed their fairy young.

As recently as 1962, a woman reported encountering a small man in green on the Berkshire Downs who appeared at her elbow when she was lost. He set her back on the correct route and then allegedly disappeared, just like that.

Another British woman claimed to have been visited by fairies all her life. Her relationship with them began during her childhood in the 1970s when she was a baby in a cot. Not yet able to speak or even comprehend what she was seeing, she said she remembered "pretty lights" dancing above her while she slept. Receiving a copy of *Flower Fairies* when she was four years old was revelatory – these "magical flying things" finally had a name. The fairies visited her less frequently as she grew up, but she said that when they did appear they were "spectacular" and recounted hanging washing in the garden with "several golden orbs dancing round in a circle". She felt a sense of magic and her senses were heightened. She also claimed the fairies spoke to her in times of need and came to her aid during dark times.

HOME HELP

Hobgoblins typically appear in British folklore and tend to live in and around the house. Once considered a "spirit of the hearth" and a helper, in more recent times the hobgoblin is considered to be a mischievous creature likely to play tricks and get up to no good.

They are usually small and hairy, resembling humans to some degree, and carry out household cleaning and chores in return for meals. They like to perform practical jokes and have a penchant for shape-shifting. Their tricks can sometimes be dangerous and they have a terrible temper. If you were to give a hobgoblin an item of clothing, this act would banish them from your house forever.

Hobgoblins are closely related to the Scottish brownie, a household spirit that comes at night and tidies the house while everyone is asleep. Brownies require an offering to be left by the hearth – usually a bowl of milk – in return for completing the chores.

They too are tricksters and if crossed will become angry and malicious. They have the power to become invisible and shape-shift into a host of different animals.

LIGHTS IN THE WOODS

In British folkore will-o'-the-wisp is a spooky blue light that shines mistily in the woods at night, usually over marsh or bog land. The haunting light tends to flicker to resemble a lantern, luring travellers from the correct path and on to treacherous ground.

Will-o'-the-wisp appears in numerous stories and legends as the representation of something the protagonist is searching for, only to lead them down a more macabre path and away from their goal.

These strange lights have been attributed to ghosts and fairies, depending on the mythos, with some believing will-o'-the-wisp is in fact a spirit that has been unable to enter either heaven or hell, and so is destined to lurk in the woods forever, misleading travellers out of vengeful rage.

Similar will-o'-the-wisp legends include the Marfa lights in Texas, the Hessdalen light in Norway, the Spooklight in Missouri and the Naga fireballs on the Mekong in Thailand.

NO HORSING AROUND

In Scottish legend, a kelpie is a malevolent water spirit, liable to shape-shift to get their own way. They are said to haunt rivers and streams and often take the form of a horse.

The kelpie may appear to children as a friendly pony, just asking to be taken for a ride. However, once the child has mounted, it will become stuck, unable to escape. Horrifyingly, once the child is secured the kelpie will take them into the river and devour them.

The kelpie also has a tendency to shape-shift into a beautiful woman with the purpose of enticing young men to their death in the water. Sometimes they assume the figure of a hairy human and hide by the water, leaping out on to unsuspecting travellers and crushing them with their incredible strength.

A kelpie boasts the strength of ten horses – a tough creature to fight. Legend has it that if you are able to take control of its bridle, you will have control of that kelpie and all of its friends. No mean feat when you can't even mount the creature for fear of being its next meal in the water, but stories speak of it having been done.

FROZEN FOREST

The wendigo is a monster said to roam the freezing forests in the northern USA and Canada. According to some stories, it's a huge creature that looms over its victims, while others describe it as human-sized, with sunken features, giant glowing yellow eyes, and sharp claws and fangs.

In some parts of North America, it is reputed to be skeletal with a heart of ice and in others it has a lipless mouth and is as tall as a tree.

A wendigo is allegedly created when someone is forced into cannibalism to survive. Centuries ago, settlers in these woods would sometimes find themselves stranded in freezing conditions and would resort to eating the dead when there was no other means of food.

Wendigos are said to be cursed to wander the forests for eternity, looking for humans to feed on and when there is nothing left to eat they will die.

GIANT BAT OF JAVA

On the Indonesian island of Java lives a giant winged creature, unidentified and yet sighted several times in the past century.

The beast, known as the Ahool, is described as being bat-like, with a body the size of a one-year-old child and a wingspan of around 3.7 m (12 ft). It has big, black eyes and is covered in short grey fur. Its face is said to be almost human-like and its wings are thick and leathery.

It is a nocturnal creature, thought to spend its days in caves behind waterfalls, and passes its nights skimming the tops of rivers hunting large fish on which to feed.

The creature is so named for its cry, which sounds like "ahool". A sighting in the 1920s left an explorer assuming there was some kind of large owl on the roof of his hut, due to the sounds penetrating through the roof, but upon investigation was shocked to discover this enormous bat-like being.

IT'S GOOD TO TALK

In the 1930s, in a tiny hamlet on the Isle of Man, lived a family who claimed to have adopted a talking pet. Their household creature Gef was a yellowish mongoose, about the size of a rat with a large bushy tail.

The family claimed that the daughter of the family had heard scratching and a voice beyond the wooden wall panels of their home. They alleged that Gef was inside and once released from the wall he spoke to them, proclaiming to have been born in New Delhi in 1852.

They said he told them he was an extremely clever mongoose, that he was an earthbound spirit in the form of the animal and apparently once announced: "I am a freak. I have hand and I have feet, and if you saw me you'd faint, you'd be petrified, mummified, turned into stone or a pillar of salt."

Gef was apparently a great help around the house, rousing family members when they overslept, acting as a sort of guard dog and warning them about approaching guests, putting out the fire at night if the family had retired and neglected to do so, and accompanying them to the market, supposedly hiding himself behind hedges and chatting all the way there. He also dealt with the mice in the house, preferring to scare them off rather than put an end to them.

The story drew great media interest, usually incorrectly referring to Gef as a "weasel" – this talking creature was a sensation in the making – but several journalists were quick to accuse the daughter of the family of ventriloquism.

Witnesses from outside the family also claimed to have heard Gef talk, but by and large the family's claims were dismissed, however several paranormal experts allegedly agreed he was likely a ghost or spirit.

SEEKING THRILLS

Pope Lick Creek in Kentucky, USA, is supposedly home to a mysterious and dangerous beast, which lurks below the trestle bridge, waiting and watching.

The Pope Lick Monster, as it is locally known, is thought to be half-human and half-goat, with short horns protruding from its forehead.

Depending on the fable, the monster allegedly uses a form of hypnosis or mimics voices to bait people on to the train tracks, where they are invariably struck by a train as there is nowhere to go other than down into the river far below. Old and rickety looking as it is, the bridge is widely thought to be out of use, when in fact this is not the case and can catch people out.

Other narratives have the monster dropping down on to car roofs from between the bridge trestles and even wielding an axe. The sight of the creature can be so horrifying that eyewitnesses are driven to jump off the bridge into the waters beneath.

One version of the story talks of the goat-man being a circus freak who escaped after being poorly treated and is angry and looking for revenge.

In 1988, a documentary about the Pope Lick Monster included scenes of people on the trestle (filmed at a separate location for safety reasons, due to the real bridge being too rickety). The film depicted a character narrowly missing being hit by a train and clinging on to the edge of the bridge. The railway company were upset at this – worried the film would encourage thrill seekers to visit and trespass on the bridge – knowing full well that it would be far more difficult to cling on to the trestle bridge at Pope Lick Creek.

Several people have died on the bridge, either after being hit by a train or falling to their death. Despite the erection of a huge fence to keep them out, legend-hunters still make the pilgrimage to Pope Lick Creek in an attempt to catch a glimpse of the notorious goat-man beneath the bridge.

SWOOPING SNALLYGASTER

In Maryland, USA, lives the local legend of the Snallygaster. This dragon-like creature is allegedly half-reptile, half-bird and has a beak full of razor-sharp teeth. Some stories claim it to have tentacles that spring from its mouth when it's ready to snatch up its prey, while others focus on its giant wingspan.

Terrifyingly, this huge beast will silently swoop down on farm animals, domestic pets and even small children, grabbing hold of them with its hook-like claws and flying off. Legend asserts the Snallygaster drinks the blood of its victims before abandoning them.

The first known sighting of the Snallygaster was back in the 1730s, but encounters with the creature were reported throughout the 1900s. A story about the being carrying off a local man and draining his blood was reported in the *Valley Register* in 1909 and the story spread and caused such a sensation that even President Theodore Roosevelt spoke about the possibility of hunting it down himself.

MAN OR BEAST?

One of historic mythology's most famous creatures is of course the Minotaur. In Greek myth the Minotaur was a monster with the body of a man, and the head and tail of a bull. He was supposedly the product of a union between the Cretan Queen Pasiphae and a bull.

Pasiphae allegedly had her way with a bull by housing herself within a wooden cow-shaped structure so as to fool it into romance. When she gave birth, she called her offspring Asterion. She was able to nurse him when he was a calf, but as he grew he became more ferocious and monster-like and started to eat people.

The Queen's husband King Minos was appalled at this reminder of his wife's beastly affair and ordered the construction of a huge maze in which to house the Minotaur.

Believed by all to be a hideous fiend, the Minotaur was ordered to exist in the labyrinth, however there was the small matter of feeding it live humans to keep it in there.

King Minos' human son had been killed and he blamed the Athenians for this. He fought against them until they agreed to pay the price for the death of his son. He demanded that once a year the Athenians give up seven young men and seven young women in order to quell the Minotaur's hunger. And so it was that the sacrificial victims made their way to Crete annually and never returned.

The third year saw Theseus, son of King Aegeus of Athens, volunteer for the annual slew of youths due to be sent into the labyrinth. His father begged him not to go, but Theseus assured him he would kill the Minotaur. He set off for Crete with black sails on his boat having promised his father he would exchange them for white sails on his return home as a sign of his victory.

Upon his arrival in Crete the daughters of King Minos allegedly fell in love with Theseus and gave him a ball of thread so that he might find his way out of the maze rather than becoming lost inside. Some versions of the story tell Theseus also stealing King Minos' sword and managing to smuggle it into the labyrinth.

Theseus made his way through the maze and eventually found the Minotaur in the furthest corner. He killed the Minotaur, either with the stolen sword or with his fists, depending on which plot variant you go with – although the sword seems more plausible when dealing with such a beast. Theseus then followed the thread that he tied to the entrance of the labyrinth and had been unravelling along his way and escaped – but not before finding the other youths and helping them escape too.

Theseus then found the king's daughters and they all sailed back to Athens together. Happily ever after, you might think, but alas... Theseus forgot to swap the black sails for white and when his father saw the dark and gloomy ship approaching assumed his son must be dead. Beside himself with grief, King Aegeus jumped into the sea, sealing his fate and giving the body of water its name – the Aegean Sea.

VAMPIRES, WEREWOLVES AND ZOMBIES

Stepping away from the world of cryptids and into the realm of "bizarre humans" brings us to the bloodsuckers, the wolf people and the flesh-devouring undead. The sensational pop culture trio of the modern age, if you will.

Learn the origins of the myths, legends and eyewitness accounts, how these creatures purportedly coexisted with humans and how history has dealt with them. Read about their legacy in modern times and how a "vampire panic" has swept across more than one community in times far more recent than you might think.

We'll look at the lesser-known wolf trials that took place alongside the better-documented witchcraft trials of centuries gone by and how the treatment of the accused left little room for a fair hearing in court.

And, last but not least, we'll journey into the world of the undead and meet the zombies from different cultures penetrating frightening folkloric tales seemingly designed to keep people in line.

NEW ENGLAND VAMPIRE HUNTERS

In the early 1800s panic swept across New England, USA. Through the states of Vermont, Maine, Massachusetts, Rhode Island and Connecticut, a vampire hunt was under way.

Whole families were dying and the villagers were at a loss to understand why. "Vampire" was the word on everyone's lips and exhumations of the dead families were very popular. Bodies were examined and often burned there in the graveyard to ensure they would not rise again. Some villages opted to simply flip the corpse over and rebury it, while others would remove the heart and torch it publicly, and some would cut straight to it and chop off the head.

Historians now know that what was in truth happening to these families was the sweep of tuberculosis – or consumption as they called it then – across whole states. Responsible for a quarter of all deaths in New England, its merciless symptoms caused village populations to dwindle.

You might think it's hardly surprising New Englanders shouted "vampire!" – tuberculosis produced a high fever, a hacking, bloody cough and the appearance as if one's life and blood had been drained from their body. This was a plague that was decimating the population and few understood what it was or how it came about. It's worth mentioning, though, that as word spread of the vampire hunting in this part of the USA, the rest of the country looked on with confusion. In an age of social and scientific progress, many thought these exhumations of bodies with wild abandon were acts of thoughtless and out-of-control superstition.

It's thought around one hundred bodies were dug up to rid the region of potential vampires and although rumours spread of the activity, it wasn't widely recorded. One accused Rhode Island vampire who did make it into the history books is Lena Brown.

In 1892 – yes, this was still going on as the century was about to turn – Lena died of consumption following the fate of her mother and sister who had succumbed to the disease a decade previously. Lena's brother was also unwell and some ne'er-do-well suggested to her father that one of the deceased female members of his family might actually be a bloodsucking vampire, feasting on his son in the night and worsening his condition. The three women were exhumed so locals could check for fresh blood in their hearts. It was winter and Lena had only died a few months previously, so her body was in good condition – and indeed there was still blood in her heart. What to do? Burn her heart and liver on a rock and feed the ashes to her sickly brother, of course.

Her exhumation and the strange ritual that followed made the press and as such was committed to history. It also enticed other writers to travel, see what they called the "New England madness" for themselves and document it.

Lena's grave can still be visited today – although the gravestone is now essentially bolted down because it's been stolen so frequently – and many make the pilgrimage to pay respects or sate their curiosity at this strange period in really quite recent history.

GLASGOW FRENZY

In 1954, children in Glasgow, Scotland, decided to take vampire hunting into their own hands. Rumours about a monster spread rapidly through the playgrounds of the city – most notably in the Gorbals, a densely populated industrial area on the edge of the Southern Necropolis – and they were determined to do something about it.

A 2 m (7 ft) vampire with iron teeth, red eyes and pale, pale skin had killed and eaten two young boys – so the children told each other – it had drained their blood and was on the prowl again. Everyone knew someone who had seen the Gorbals Vampire, who allegedly lived in the graveyard, or had more information about it, or knew the kids who had met their grisly end. The children worked themselves into a frenzy and hatched a plan.

On September 23, when the school bell rang, around 400 kids descended on the Southern Necropolis to hunt out the bloodsucking monster. Tiny, pre-school-aged infants toddled along with their bigger siblings and the oldest – leaders of the gang – were 14 years old. Armed with penknives, sticks, stones and crucifixes, they headed into the graveyard to seek out the vampire.

The children darted about in a frantic attack mode, climbing over and peering around the huge and elaborate Victorian tombs.

Adding to the atmosphere was the end-of-days-style backdrop of the local steelworks, from which flames jumped and smoke billowed. The smell of sulphur hung in the air.

It was a moody scene – and one which the police found themselves unable to control. Upon their arrival at the graveyard the children informed the police that they had to kill the vampire with the iron teeth who lived among the tombs – for he had killed two of the city's children. The chaos only abated when the local headmaster was called on to restore some order. Some of the children returned the next day and for three nights sought out their bloodsucking prey.

The adults blamed American horror comics such as *Tales from the Crypt* and *Dark Mysteries* (which actually featured a story in December 1953 titled "The Vampire with the Iron Teeth") – passed around the schoolyard and discussed excitedly by the children – for the rampage to the hunt down the Gorbals Vampire. The teachers' union, Christian groups and the Communist Party worked together to clamp down on what they called "harmful publications", and 1955 saw the introduction of the Children and Young Persons (Harmful Publications) Act which protects under-18s from "any book, magazine or other like work which is likely to fall into the hands of children or young persons" featuring "the commission of crimes; or acts of violence or cruelty; or incidents of a repulsive or horrible nature; in such a way that the work as a whole would tend to corrupt a child or young person into whose hands it might fall." The Act specifically references comics and is still in place today.

No evidence of two missing schoolboys from that time has ever been unearthed and yet the children believed. On September 26, 1954, the *Sunday Mail* published a story with the headline "Vampire with iron teeth is 'dead'".

STAKINGS IN SERBIA

In the early 1700s, in the depths of rural Serbia a man came back from the dead.

Ten weeks after his funeral, Peter Plogojowitz allegedly returned home to his wife. She claimed he appeared at the door and asked for his shoes; petrified, she handed them to him and he left quietly.

Over the next few days nine people came forward to report being attacked by Plogojowitz, swearing that he had strangled them until they were almost dead, and fed on them while they slipped in and out of consciousness. He had supposedly sucked blood from their throat or stomach and now, as they reported this horrendous attack, they were weak and pale. All nine people died within 24 hours of their encounter.

Plogojowitz appeared to his wife once more and was aggressive, demanding she give him food. She hid, while her adult son refused his undead father entry to their home. Plogojowitz attacked his son and killed him. His wife fled the village, convinced she would be his next victim.

The villagers demanded action and insisted the body of Plogojowitz be exhumed to be analyzed for proof and destroyed. The official assigned the task oversaw the unearthing of Plogojowitz's coffin and was startled by what he found inside. The body had not decayed but looked healthy and plump. He looked rather pale, but astonishingly some of his skin appeared to be peeling away to reveal new rosy skin underneath. Plogojowitz's beard had grown since death and his fingernails had not only continued their growth, but had shed and regrown, the old ones found loose in the bottom of the coffin. A few drops of dried blood were dotted around his mouth.

The villagers stepped in and drove a metal stake into the dead man's heart. Allegedly, fresh blood appeared from the wound, as well as from his ears, nose and mouth. Plogojowitz's body was then burned to ashes, just to be sure.

Only a few years later in another Serbian village, an even deadlier vampire came to light. According to his own testimony, Arnold Paole was serving in the military when he was attacked by an undead monster. He was so shaken by his experience, he tracked down the perpetrator to their grave, exhumed the body and decapitated it. In an attempt to protect himself further, he wiped blood from the creature over his skin and ate some of the soil around the grave.

However, tragically, Paole died – and then came back. Villagers who had known Paole started reporting seeing him walking through the streets at night, while at the same time sheep were dying mysteriously. Four people said they had been attacked by him. The villagers knew the story of Plogojowitz and what had to be done if they were to stay safe. They dug up his body and were horrified to find a fresh-blood-soaked corpse, crimson running from his eyes, nose and mouth. As they drove a stake through his heart he groaned and rose but the villagers were ready and torched him then and there in his coffin.

The four villagers who had been attacked and subsequently died were also unearthed and given the same five-star vampire treatment.

Vampire activity quietened down for a while, but resumed again a few years later. Serbians felt this to be an ongoing battle, but after yet more exhumations, stakings and burnings they were becoming pros when it came to vampire hunting and all went quiet on the bloodsucking front for good.

SELF-EATING VAMP

In German legend, the Nachzehrer is a type of vampire living predominantly in the northern areas of the country. It is unusual in vampire terms in that once it has turned, it eats its own burial shroud and then starts to consume its own flesh. The act of eating itself supposedly guarantees survival, but weakens its living family members and once the Nachzehrer has finished its self-meal it moves on to them.

It is apparently rather noisy – with table manners that leave a lot to be desired – and if you were passing a grave containing one, you would be able to hear it eating itself. This curious creature can apparently be identified in its coffin by its unusual position, holding one thumb in the other hand and always keeping its left eye open.

One does not become a Nachzehrer through an attack, biting or scratching, but it is thought to be the fate for suicide victims or the first to die of a plague.

Variants on the legend involve the Nachzehrer's ability to shape-shift into a pig to do its blood-draining of family and friends. Others suggest it is able to scale the local church tower to ring the bells and all who hear them will die.

Nachzehrers can be terminated via the usual method of decapitation or burning and some have suggested burying the deceased with a stone in their mouth to prevent the self-eating from ever commencing.

BLOODSUCKING INSPIRATION

The most famous vampire of all is of course Dracula, created by Irish author Bram Stoker in 1897. The eponymous novel (which was originally called *The Dead Undead*), told through diary entries, letters and newspaper articles, is the Gothic tale of Count Dracula, a vampire living in a castle in Transylvania, Romania, who leaves his home for Whitby in the UK in order to wreak his bloodsucking havoc around the northern seaside town.

Since the release of the novel, vampirism has steadily flooded into popular culture – at times to the point of saturation – with films, books, comics, games and TV shows in abundance. Think *The Munsters, Dark Shadows, Interview With the Vampire, From Dusk 'til Dawn, Buffy the Vampire Slayer, 30 Days of Night, Twilight, True Blood* and *The Vampire Diaries* to name only a brief selection of the most popular to make it to the screen. It's fair to say the vampire discourse has well and truly sunk its teeth into the public consciousness.

Of course, Dracula wasn't dreamt up without plenty of inspiration from abroad. For starters there were the myths, legends and vampire panics of previous centuries, but Stoker also borrowed several aspects from the life of Romanian tyrant Vlad the Impaler – so named for his preferred method of ending his victims.

Vlad was a prince who lived in Transylvania. He was the only surviving member of his family, who were brutally murdered, and his surname was Draculea (*drac* meaning "dragon"). Vlad became the ruler of Wallachia, a principality in modern-day Romania, and found himself presiding over a slew of quarrelsome landowners and aristocrats. He invited hundreds of them to a banquet where he ordered them to be stabbed and then impaled each of them – of course he did.

Stories of Vlad's cruel and sadistic nature spread across Europe. He allegedly impaled a troop of warriors and then sat down to dine, while they writhed on their poles, slowly dying. Other stories recount how he liked to dip his bread in the blood of his victims.

In total he is estimated to have killed around 80,000 people through cruel, cold, calculating and gruesome means. He was captured and beheaded in 1476, and his head delivered to one of his enemies to be displayed above the city gates.

Suitably bloody inspiration for the inception of the Prince of Darkness, I think you'll agree.

MURDER ON THE DANCE FLOOR

The Pishacha is a vampire-like creature from Hindu legend. These dreadful beings have bulging red eyes and pulsing veins protruding all over their body. They only come out at night and tend to roam graveyards and places where there has been violent death. The modern take on the Pishacha sees it haunt nightclubs and bars, feeding on negative energy and preying on the weak.

They can shape-shift into any living form or to make themselves invisible to the human eye. They can possess the mind of their victim, controlling their thoughts and behaviour usually to the point of insanity and feeding on the misery that ensues.

The Pishacha feeds on human flesh and blood and is believed to possess its own language – paisaci. In Hinduism it is believed that certain mantras can protect people from being assaulted or possessed by the Pishacha and during religious festivals they are given various offerings to keep them content and away.

WOLVES OF THE MIDWEST

Across the Midwestern states of the USA, notably Michigan and Wisconsin, local fables thrive about wolf-like creatures prowling the woods at night.

The Michigan Dogman is allegedly a 2.1 m (7 ft) dog-human hybrid, with yellow eyes, the head of a wolf or dog, the torso of a man and a howl that sounds like a human scream. If you believe the stories, the dogman only makes an appearance once a decade, in years that end with a seven. The creature is usually spotted in north-western Michigan around the Manistee River, which flows into Lake Michigan.

The first sighting of the Michigan Dogman was in 1887, when two lumberjacks reported seeing the creature in the woods. Other sightings followed – although presumably only in years ending with a seven – often from men working in the woods or people walking on solitary roads and many of these reports originated in the logging camps in the area.

People talk of the dogman's agility and many have seen it bound around. Some have even claimed it has jumped in front of them or their car, or that it has scratched at a house or tent while they were inside.

Amateur video footage from the 1970s shows what the creators claim to be true sightings of the dogman moving through the woods. Although in both instances these were deemed to be faked, believers can't shake the fact that the way the large creature moves in both clips is so naturally wolf-like that they're not sure it could be emulated by a human in a dog suit.

In neighbouring Wisconsin, the so-called Beast of Bray Road supposedly terrorizes several counties. It's described as a man-wolf or dogman, with a muscular human-like body with a wolf's head and legs – it also has yellow eyes. Could the Michigan Dogman have crossed the border?

The beast was first sighted in 1936 – perhaps it holidays in Michigan when the year ends with a seven? – but reports really picked up in the 1980s and 90s. Those claiming to have spotted the beast say they have seen it eating its kill by the side of the road or in the forest, either on its haunches or kneeling in a human-like fashion. No one has been attacked, but they have witnessed aggressive behaviour, with some claiming to have been chased or had the creature jump on their car.

There is photographic evidence of the supposed beast and one local newspaper picked up the story when the number of sightings peaked in the early 1990s. The journalist was hugely sceptical, but reluctantly agreed to cover the story. After delving into the evidence and interviewing various eyewitnesses, she became convinced of the beast's existence and even wrote a book about it! If you're asking, look no further than *The Beast of Bray Road: Tailing Wisconsin's Werewolf*.

WOLF TRIALS

Just as there were ruthless and unsparing witch trials, many innocents across Europe were accused of werewolf activity and also executed unjustly.

Similarly to the accused witches, suspected werewolves were thought to have made a pact with the Devil or to be influenced by his power in some way. And much like the witchcraft trials, there were also confessions – with one man claiming he had a magical belt that, when he wore it, allowed him to transform into a wolf. Another claimed to have been given this shape-shifting power by the Devil and that he worked with ten other wolves doing his bidding – which mainly entailed killing livestock and spreading general chaos.

These accusations of lycanthropy (werewolfery) were also lumped in with claims of wolf-riding and wolf-charming, both of which were also considered to be on the dark side of the law. If found guilty, the accused would be charged with witchcraft and likely hanged and then burned at the stake, just to make sure.

A FAMILY OF WOLVES

In 1598, an entire family were accused of lycanthropy in Jura, France.

A brother and sister were picking fruit when a wolf emerged from the bushes and grabbed the young girl. In order to protect his sister, the young boy drew a knife, but the wolf fought back and barged him, driving the knife into the boy's neck. Some locals heard the fray and fought the wolf, injuring it, and were able to chase it until it limped away.

The brother and sister died of their injuries, but before they perished the boy was able to describe his assailant. He said the wolf had hands like a human, though covered in fur.

A local woman, Perrenette Gandillon, appeared to display a new injury – a wound in the very place the wolf had been struck. Witch-hunter extraordinaire Henri Boguet had been among the crowd that fought the wolf that day and nursed a personal vendetta. He rallied a mob, who sought out Perrenette and executed her.

There were rumours among the local people that the Gandillon family practised witchcraft, so they were all hastily arrested. Perrenette's daughter confessed, but her brother and son held back. They were imprisoned and observed, and this is when Boguet witnessed their startling behaviour. They crawled around on all fours, and barked and howled at each other, their bodies covered in mysterious scratches.

When questioned about their behaviour they eventually confessed to doing the Devil's work and the rest of the Gandillon family were burned at the stake.

Boguet was a ruthless man of the law, claiming to have tried and executed some 600 werewolves during his career as grand justice of the district. He wrote prolifically on the subject and his book *Discours Exécrable des Sorciers* (loosely translating as *An Examen of Witches*), first released in 1602, was reprinted 12 times in 20 years due to its popularity.

REIGN OF TERROR

In the late 1500s, Peter Stubbe (also known in some sources as Stumpp) wreaked lycanthropic terror across western Germany. Modern commentators refer to Stubbe as a ruthless serial killer, murdering as many as 18 people, but there's no getting away from the fact that 400 years ago he was accused of witchcraft, cannibalism and werewolf activity.

Stubbe's case was recorded in a 16-page pamphlet, an English translation of which survives and can be found in the British Library. A rare comprehensive insight into these allegations of lycanthropy and witchcraft many hundreds of years ago.

Stubbe claimed he had made a pact with Satan, who granted him the power to transform into a werewolf whenever he pleased. He was a wretched character who would apparently tip his hat politely to locals in the street and then rape or murder them later. If anyone crossed him, or even so much as caught his eye, they were unlikely to live to tell the tale.

He was known to rape women in his human form, before shape-shifting to wolf mode to kill them, and would often partially devour his victims. He killed countless women and children, and even attacked and slaughtered his own kin – allegedly luring his own son into the forest, killing him and eating his brains. A cold and calculating psychopath.

Stubbe's reign of terror lasted for 25 years, despite many attempting to track down this killer wolf-man. He was eventually cornered by a mob when in wolf form and dogs were set upon him. He transformed back to his human shape in front of the crowd, who were struck dumb at the sight of the friendly local they knew.

He was imprisoned and put on trial, where he confessed to a multitude of sordid and inhumane acts and was sentenced to a horrible death, which involved prolonged torture, before he was beheaded and his remains burned at the stake.

FULL-MOON THEORY

The theory that werewolves only appear under a full moon is rooted in the idea that this type of moon influences regular wolves' behaviour and that they supposedly howl at it. When it comes to regular wolves, any evidence for this conduct is purely anecdotal.

When it comes to humans, however, there are a lot of firm believers that the moon controls the tides, but its force has been deemed too weak to do anything else. But this won't stop people believing. A whopping 40 studies have been carried out into the "lunar effect" – the purported theory that the lunar cycle impacts human behaviour – and they all reported no connection. The only explanation offered was that full-moonlit nights were brighter – especially in an era with no streetlights – and so perhaps wayward night-time behaviour was planned around the giant nightlight in the sky so people could actually see what they were doing. Still, believers gonna believe.

Back to the legend. The first full moon of the year is referred to as a "wolf moon" because many believe it is the moon most likely to turn someone into a werewolf. The power of this moon can supposedly transform humans predisposed to werewolfery into super-wolves. According to legend, the wolf moon is the most dangerous of the year, when usually solitary werewolves form packs to go hunting.

Werewolves first appeared in ancient Greek myth – Lycaon got on the wrong side of Zeus so he turned him into a wolf. The oldest documented account of a man transforming into a wolf features in the poem *Epic of Gilgamesh*, which dates back to 2100 BC.

DON'T MESS WITH THE LAW

The city of Ansbach in Bavaria, Germany, harbours a bloody tale of seventeenth-century lycanthropy. In 1685, when an unusual number of farm animals and livestock were found dead or missing, the locals suspected wolves to be at work, but when the residents themselves started turning up dead or going AWOL they suspected something more sinister.

The chief magistrate of the city had been a cruel and merciless man and his death not long before these wolf-like slayings led some to believe he might have returned to wreak bloody havoc across the community who – due to the fact he was so unpleasant in life – had not mourned his passing.

Moving on from the animals, the creature began to attack those who tended them, favouring women and children who lived on the farms as his victims.

The lupine creature was eventually tracked down and a heady chase ensued. It didn't give up easily and a mob of townspeople and hounds pursued it for many miles. Eventually it grew weary and jumped into a well to hide. With nowhere to run, the mob attacked it with pitchforks, rocks and anything they could lay their hands on. The creature eventually met its end and died in the well.

Unusually for werewolf stories, the creature did not revert to human form upon its death, but instead remained in its wolf state. The people of Ansbach were utterly convinced this wolf was in fact the resurrection of the cruel magistrate and so treated the wolf as if it were human. They paraded the beast through the city streets, dressed in human clothing and adding a beard and wig so it resembled the dead magistrate. Following the parade, the wolf was hung in a public place for all to see – presumably as a warning to anyone else considering werewolf behaviour – and eventually preserved and placed in a museum.

WOLF OF MONTANA

In 2018, a farmer in rural Montana, USA, shot and killed a wolf-like beast threatening cows on his land. He called the authorities to report the incident, but when they arrived they found something else altogether.

The beast looked like a wolf, but it had long, grey fur, long claws and a huge head. The official present from the Fish, Wildlife and Parks department claimed its big, floppy ears were much too large and its legs too short for it to be a common wolf or dog. Its teeth and paws were also far too short.

One theory suggested the creature was a dire wolf, a sabre-toothed canine creature that once lived in North America but has been extinct for at least 10,000 years. Another thought it could be a *shunka warakin* – a wolf–hyena hybrid hailing from Native American folklore that has a penchant for cattle; its name translates as "carries off dogs", which gives you an idea of what it's capable of. Another shouted the inevitable "werewolf!". While someone wondered if it might be a sasquatch baby.

Whatever they found, it baffled the authorities and whipped up a storm of excitement among the cryptid-loving community.

REMORSEFUL TEENAGER

One of the youngest people ever accused of and executed for werewolf activity is Estonia's Hans the Werewolf, who was just 18 years old.

Accusations of witchcraft were rife in the Baltic region in the 1600s. Many people practised paganism and folk magic often went hand in hand. Ignorance was rife among the authorities, who assumed anything even vaguely resembling magic was an act of satanic worship and the perpetrator must be in league with the Devil.

Hans was taken in for questioning following reports of unusual behaviour – it didn't take much for someone to be nabbed in an era of everlasting investigations of demonic conduct and the torture of suspects that was so severe they eventually confessed to some form of witchcraft.

However, Hans answered truthfully with no need for torture. Despite there being no evidence of human death at his hand, he admitted in court to shape-shifting into a werewolf and going hunting for at least the past two years. He claimed he had not wanted to transform and had no power over the change from human to wolf. He alleged that a man dressed in black had bitten him and upon learning this man was a werewolf had understood the affliction he now possessed. He showed the court a scar that looked like a dog bite, alleging this to be from the wolf-man in black.

The court officials were intrigued at this opportunity to hear a werewolf speak candidly about his condition while in human form and questioned him thoroughly. Hans talked about how he felt while he was a werewolf, that the transformation was spiritual as well as physical and at that time he felt more like a beast than a man.

Despite the lack of evidence of any murder, the bite he received from the man in black was interpreted as a demonic pact and Hans was sent to his death.

Many believed Hans was a teenage boy telling a story to evade the likely hideous torture that awaited him. However, others thought his words too convincing and explanations too vivid for it all to be a teenage fantasy.

HOLD YOUR BREATH

In Chinese legend, a Jiangshi – which translates as "stiff corpse" – is said to be created upon death when a person's soul fails to leave its host's body. This punishment given to the deceased supposedly happens when the person has been badly behaved or unpleasant to others in life.

This undead creature has pasty skin and green mossy patches growing on its flesh, as well as a very long tongue and sharp, black fingernails. In classic zombie fashion it supposedly wanders about with its arms stretched in front and is blind, so if you hold your breath and stay very quiet it might just pass you by.

One version of the story sees the Jiangshi raised by a necromancer – for laughs, one assumes – while others talk of improper death or failure to bury the body following the funeral being the cause. The latter explanation apparently also requires a bolt of lightning to strike the corpse or a pregnant cat to jump over its coffin.

Like all creatures, the Jiangshi has its weak spots and can be caught out if you know how to handle it. It isn't a fan of small, scattered objects – much like the traditional vampire – so be sure to scatter some rice about to distract it. It will apparently withdraw if it hears a rooster's call and something made from the wood of a peach tree might just ward it off. It's also worth trying a mirror, vinegar, adzuki beans, an axe, the hooves of a black donkey or blood of a black dog, should you have those to hand.

SHOEMAKER OF BRESLAU

In the 1500s in Breslau, Poland, legend has it a dead shoemaker came back to haunt the town. The shoemaker slit his own throat and, despite a proper burial, was seen by several of the townspeople a few weeks later.

He was spotted in the daytime as well as at night. The public refused to believe these people had really seen a dead man walking the streets, but when several others reported being assaulted by him too, the majority began to pay attention. The attacks were unusual in that the shoemaker would lie on top of them and crush them with his heavy weight. Some descriptions claim he was a vampire, draining the blood from his victims and leaving them for dead.

After several months of these molestations, the town authorities bowed to the pressure of its residents and exhumed the shoemaker's body. They found it had not decayed and that it was supple – most unusual for a corpse. Skin had peeled away and new skin had grown underneath it. His body was displayed in the town and people came to view it, as you do. The attacks continued after the unearthing of the body, so it was buried under the gallows. This did nothing to stop the dead shoemaker and he was dug up – only to appear plumper and healthier than ever – cut into bits, burned to ashes and dumped into the river.

GREEK UNDEAD

A chilling Greek legend concerns the walking dead. The Vrykolakas supposedly rise from their graves and walk the streets knocking on people's doors. One can become a Vrykolakas following sinful behaviour through life, religious banishment, burial in unholy ground or through eating the meat of a sheep that has been attacked by a werewolf.

Vrykolakas do not decay, but do grow to be very large, with a rosy, plump complexion as if alive and healthy. They display a variety of behaviours, such as wandering about at night causing mischief, to poltergeist-like activity and allegedly spreading epidemics within the local living community. In some stories they eat flesh and make a beeline for their victim's liver, and legend states they have been known to crush unlucky people in the night, suffocating them while they sleep.

The creatures supposedly have an agenda, seeking out the home of their victim, knocking on the door and saying their name aloud. If the resident were to open the door after the first knock, they would be cursed and would die a few days later, turning into a Vrykolakas upon their demise. If there was no answer after the first knock, they would be spared. This is where the rural Greek superstition comes from – many people do not answer the door after their visitor first knocks but wait for them to pause and knock again.

In order to rid oneself of a Vrykolakas, one must wait until Saturday – the only day or night where they don't rise from their graves – and unbury and destroy the body through beheading, decapitation and cremation. This is also considered a service to the Vrykolakas as well as its future victims, the act of freeing it from living death.

During the Second World War, the Great Famine of 1941–2 saw 300,000 starve and perish. The graveyards were full, leading to mass burials on unconsecrated ground, which families feared would mean their loved ones were likely to return as Vrykolakas. Many went so far as to behead deceased family members in order to spare them this undead return.

A HISTORY OF ZOMBIES

Zombies have been almost omnipresent in the past decade or so, their popularity increasing ever since George A. Romero's classic *Night of the Living Dead* (1968) and *Dawn of the Dead* (1978) movies. In more recent years, comic-book-adapted TV show *The Walking Dead* pulled in more than 17 million viewers at its peak and ran for a whopping 12 years; and big-hitters such as *Resident Evil*, *28 Days Later*, *Shaun of the Dead*, *World War Z*, *Zombieland* and *Train to Busan*, to name a few, have racked up the dollars at the box office and commanded various sequels.

The term "zombie" as we know it today was first used in Romero's second outing, *Dawn of the Dead*, and from then on no one has held back, but the origin of this word for the undead stretches back much further to Haiti in the seventeenth century, when it was called Saint-Domingue under French rule. Haitian slaves believed that when they died they would be free in the afterlife to return home; but if they were to take their own life – as many did, because they were treated so inhumanely and worked to the brink of death, if not actually death – their soul would become trapped in their body and they would be forced to wander the plantations as a slave for eternity.

The Haitian Revolution of 1804 heralded the end of French colonialism in the Caribbean and the evolution of the zombie legend. Haitians began to believe that zombies were in fact dead people who could be reanimated by voodoo priests or shamans. Despite the abolition of slavery, they believed those who practised the dark arts would bewitch the undead and have them do their bidding – sometimes using their zombie slaves for free labour.

Zombies first appeared on screen in Victor Halperin's *White Zombie* in 1932 – which stars Bela Lugosi, most famous for playing Dracula, but that's another story – in which the undead featured fit into the Haitian and voodoo stories.

GALVANIZING THE DEAD

In the eighteenth century in Victorian London, there was a roaring trade in dead bodies. The study of anatomy had become a requirement for anyone wishing to practise medicine, but the lack of bodies on which to practise became a problem. There were no fridges or freezers in which to keep dead bodies "fresh", so the turnover was pretty high.

Grave robbers, known as "resurrection men", would pilfer just-buried bodies from cemeteries and sell them to private medical schools for dissection. The Victorian trend for elaborate tombs and mausoleums was designed to offer those who had the money an escape from having their grave rummaged through. An adult corpse could fetch £10, which is around £800 in today's money. It was a lucrative business. At this time, executed murderers were denied a burial under law and so their bodies were also handed over to science.

Medical schools found the bodies were piling up. This offered ample opportunity for much dissection and exploration of the human body – which is one of the reasons why there was a big leap forward in medical understanding at the time. It also offered something to the public.

The medical schools started staging post-mortem dissections to a morbidly fascinated public audience (this being a pre-TV age of course).

New-found knowledge of the inside of the human body brought with it interest in other areas of death. Medical practitioners began to experiment with electricity to ascertain what a dead body could achieve if a current was passed through various bits of it. Public demonstrations took place that saw freshly hanged people reanimated through this method, called galvanization.

In previous decades, eminent scientists – one of them Luigi Galvani, from whom galvanization gets its name – had experimented with electricity and dead animals, to great acclaim. Lectures were held on the topic and were well-attended – one young woman in the audience by the name of Mary Godwin (who became Mary Shelley) would be inspired by such events to write *Frankenstein*.

The College of Surgeons in London invited Giovanni Aldini to carry out his galvanic experiments to an audience. Aldini claimed he had once placed two severed heads of dead criminals on separate tables and connected them via an arc of electricity so they contorted and pulled faces at a crowd of terrified spectators.

The purpose of Aldini's invitation to the college was to galvanize recently deceased murderer George Foster. Foster was hanged and left where he died for an hour in winter temperatures of -2°C. Foster was laid out in front of an audience while Aldini performed his electrical experiments for around seven hours. By applying arcs of electricity to different parts of Foster's body he was able to make the corpse "perform". To the crowd's shock, one eye opened, his jaw shuddered and his face convulsed. Further currents applied to his body caused a hand to clench, which delighted all the morbidly fascinated in the room.

KEEPING WATCH

In Norse mythology the undead are said to live on in their graves to guard treasure that has been buried alongside them. Unlike in vampire legend in which the protagonist stays plump and healthy long after death, the Draugar is a rotting, hideous creature that gives off a foul odour. It is described as having blue skin and supposedly possesses superhuman strength. It can be identified by a bright light glowing from its burial mound – a fire that supposedly forms a barrier between the lands of the living and the dead.

Although most – and presumably once very wealthy – Draugar will stay close to their burial mound in order to protect their earthly goods, in some Nordic countries they are also noted for their magical abilities, such as soothsaying, controlling the weather and shape-shifting. In Icelandic legend it is the Draugar that takes the form of the "seal with human-like eyes" said to be responsible for shipwrecks and death at sea. There are also tales of it transforming into a cat that will sit on its victim's chest while they are asleep and slowly grow heavier until they have suffocated the person underneath them.

Quite terrifying and in the vein of Freddy Krueger, they are also able to enter your dreams while you slumber – and they'll leave a gift behind just so you can rest easy knowing your vision has been intruded upon. They also have the ability to spread disease across a community, turn the day to night and inflict curses upon their victims.

Spending eternity as a Draugar is believed to be the fate for anyone who is unpleasant or greedy in life and their protection of their grave treasure is fierce – they will violently attack anyone who attempts to rob their final resting place. Besides a fire at the burial mound, in some stories the Draugar can be identified in their grave if the corpse is found to be upright or in a seated position.

These beasts possess such strength and power that they can be hard to dispose of, but the usual beheading, chopping into little pieces, burning and chucking in the sea usually does the job.

ALIENS
AND UFOs

We've all caught sight of a strange light in the sky, perhaps something moving across the darkness at a pace we don't recognize. More often than not we realize it's a plane, a satellite or a fiery paper lantern floating in the heavens. But, admit it, your brain whispers "UFO" if only for a nanosecond. Whether we believe or not, the idea of spaceships, UFOs and intelligent life visiting us from other planets is so deeply rooted in our popular culture that it's hard not to let our minds go there.

In this chapter we will tell the stories of those who claim to have had encounters with spacecraft or interplanetary beings. It's one thing to spot some strange lights in the sky but quite another to happen upon a fully functioning spacecraft in a forest clearing and watch as an extraterrestrial creature steps out of it – and possibly attempts to drag you on board.

It's up to you whether you believe the stories, but they certainly offer food for thought.

ROSWELL REVISITED

Arguably the most famous of all UFO encounters, Roswell is synonymous with alien conspiracies. The term "flying saucer" had been coined by the press only a few weeks before, in June 1947, when a pilot flying close to Mount Rainier in Washington state, USA, had spotted nine distant objects crossing the sky in formation. He had described them as being "shaped like a pie plate" and "saucer-like", and had unwittingly kicked off UFO fever.

So, in July, around 170 km (75 miles) outside the town of Roswell, New Mexico, when a farmer found a host of unusual objects in his sheep field, he jumped to extraterrestrial conclusions. Among the debris were metal rods held together with tape, chunks of plastic and foil. After reporting the incident to the local police department, soldiers from the nearby Roswell Army Air Field (RAAF) base promptly appeared, cleared up the mysterious detritus and whisked it away. They later issued a press release announcing they had recovered a "flying disc".

However, the RAAF were quick to retract their statement and instead claimed the wreckage discovered on the farmland had actually been that of a weather balloon rather than an alien spacecraft. The seed had already been planted, though, and many suspected a cover-up. Mystery and controversy have surrounded the town of Roswell ever since, and in more recent years "evidence" has come to light in the form of witness statements and even snippets of supposed alien autopsy footage.

Thanks in no small part to Charles Berlitz and William Moore's book *The Roswell Incident*, published in 1980 and drawing on eyewitness accounts, the incident became the stuff of pop cultural legend. Present-day Roswell is awash with alien-themed restaurants, bars and hotels, not to mention museums, gift shops and – the jewel in its crown – a McDonald's shaped like a spaceship. Striking numbers of "believers" flock to the town's alien conventions and UFO festival annually, having made Roswell their spiritual home.

CROP CIRCLES: FACT OR FICTION?

Patterns have been appearing in farmers' fields for hundreds of years; elaborate, impressive, huge and often beautiful, many would call them works of art, almost otherworldly in nature. The formations appear in fields of grain or corn, where the crops have been flattened to create the display and had long been thought to be the work of extraterrestrial beings – perhaps using strong air currents to beat down the plants.

In the seventeenth century, some thought crop circles to be the work of the Devil, however in more recent times the believers are clear on them being the work of creatures from outer space.

The term "crop circle" was coined in the early 1980s after a spate of formations appeared in the 1970s and popularized the idea that alien forces were at play. South West England has long been the hotspot for the appearance of these elaborate patterns, but similar circular formations have also been discovered in swamp reeds and sugarcane fields in Australia, and grain fields in Canada.

In 1991 two British men came forward and admitted they were responsible for hundreds of crop circles created in the South West since 1978. They claimed to have used planks of wood and rope to flatten the crops, and loops of wire to help them walk in straight lines. To prove it, they created one of their now-famous circles in front of journalists and called upon an expert to assess it, pretending it was a new discovery. The expert deemed it to be the real deal, before they were informed it was created by human hands.

There were plenty of instances of crop circles elsewhere in the world, but it was thought that the two British men had sparked an army of copycat crop circle-makers, who have only grown more skilled and begun to create more sophisticated formations over the years. And crop formations are even used for elaborate marketing campaigns – with the Olympic rings and Star Wars Rebel Alliance emblem just two examples.

While the scientists claim they are all man-made and the work of dedicated hoaxers, true believers claim there are real formations amid the fakes and that they can tell the difference. Some think crop circles are created by lightning strikes so powerful that they must be controlled by something; while others believe they are created by spaceships and are a sign of otherworldly beings attempting to communicate with us on Earth.

CELESTIAL SPECTACLE

In the 1560s in Nuremberg – now part of Germany, but then an independent city-state in the Holy Roman Empire – city dwellers were treated to an out-of-this-world light show.

They watched in awe as the sky lit up with unusual objects darting around in what they described as a "battle". According to eyewitness reports, the objects were shaped like triangles, spheres, crosses, cylinders, spears and moons. They moved at great speed, dodging and crashing into one another, until there was a huge bang and the sky fell quiet.

The incident over Nuremberg is considered the largest mass sighting of its kind, witnessed as it was by countless residents looking up from the city below. A woodcut engraving from the time featured a description of the remarkable incident:

They all started to fight among themselves, so that the globes, which were first in the sun, flew out to the ones standing on both sides, thereafter, the globes standing outside the sun, in the small and large rods, flew into the sun.

Besides the globes flew back and forth among themselves and fought vehemently with each other for over an hour. And when the conflict in and again out of the sun was most intense, they became fatigued to such an extent that they all, as said above, fell from the sun down upon the earth 'as if they all burned' and they then wasted away on the earth with immense smoke.

HONEYMOON ABDUCTION

In September 1961, in the mountains of New Hampshire, USA, unassuming couple Barney and Betty Hill were driving home from their honeymoon in Niagara Falls. They spotted a strange light in the sky that appeared to be following them. The light zigzagged across the road, disappearing behind trees and mountain ridges only to reappear again. They stopped by the side of the road and observed through binoculars what Betty described as an object spinning in the night sky.

They returned home, but by this point it was dawn and several hours had passed without their realizing. They both felt a sense of unease as well as an overwhelming dread they had forgotten something. During the course of the evening, their watches had stopped working, and Betty found that her dress was ripped, while Barney's shoes were scuffed. In the time that followed, Barney suffered from physical aches and pains, and Betty experienced unsettling dreams.

Betty called the local US Air Force base to report the sighting of the spinning disc, but it was decided what she and Barney had actually spotted was the planet Jupiter. So, in an attempt to understand what they had seen and experienced, Betty found a book on UFOs and wrote to its author. He suggested hypnosis might help the couple to get to the bottom of their mysterious encounter.

After several months of hypnosis sessions, the findings were remarkable. Barney and Betty were assessed separately, and both recalled being led from the road and on to a spaceship by short, pale-grey creatures with large eyes set in an oversized head. Their description would cement this depiction of aliens in popular culture for decades to come. They said the extra-terrestrials wore military uniforms and went on to describe the medical examinations they were subject to aboard the craft.

As well as providing a rough sketch of the spaceship itself, Betty also drew a star map she claimed to have seen during the abduction. Experts thought this could possibly be an interpretation of obscure star system Zeta Reticuli, which can only be seen from Earth in very dark skies.

The Hills' experience was one of many to be investigated by the secretive US government arm Project Blue Book – which compiled and recorded official inquiries into more than 12,000 UFO sightings from its inception in 1952 until it was disbanded in 1969.

The couple collaborated with writer John Fuller to tell their story in his bestselling 1966 book *An Interrupted Journey*, which should you be so inclined features the verbatim scripts of their hypnosis sessions.

GOLDEN STATE FLAP

In extraterrestrial terminology, a "flap" is a series of similar sightings of UFOs in the same area over a short period of time.

One famous flap occurred toward the end of 1896 over California, USA, when reports streamed in of "mystery airships" spotted in the sky at night. Eyewitnesses described vast crafts that could travel at great speed, while others claimed to have glimpsed the occupants whom they thought were human but displayed unusual clothing and behaviour. Strange lights in the sky were also oft reported in 1896–7 and in the age before commercial flight, this was taken rather more seriously by both the public and officials.

Newspapers splashed stories across their front pages with headlines shouting "AS LARGE AS A BIG WHALE" and "STRANGE CRAFT OF THE SKY". Reporters liked to speculate that the airships were from Mars or Venus.

Science fiction writers of the time such as H. G. Wells and Jules Verne spun tales of submarines, airships and extraterrestrial forces – although it is undecided as to whether the sightings of the mystery airships of the late 1800s influenced their work or vice versa.

LATE CHRISTMAS VISITORS

In the early hours of Boxing Day 1980, in remote Rendlesham Forest in Suffolk, UK, several witnesses claimed to have seen some unusual festive guests among the trees.

US Air Force security guards on patrol from the nearby Royal Air Force (RAF) base reported strange red lights in the woods and upon further investigation discovered what they believed to be a triangular spacecraft in a clearing on the forest floor.

One witness stated that the craft or its inhabitants broadcasted numbers directly into his brain, before it rose into the air and departed at great speed. The police were called and found what could have been landing marks on the ground and broken branches alerting them to the presence of a heavy object.

Incredibly, later that evening, the security personnel reported yet more lights in the forest and believed the spacecraft had returned. They found more damage to foliage, as well as scorch marks. After hours of keeping watch, in the early hours of the following morning a light was observed along the tree line of the woods. The security team pursued the light for quite a while, claiming to have seen changing, bright colours as it moved across the sky, skirting the tips of the trees. They recorded their pursuit of the craft and 20 minutes of this is available online, should you fancy a listen to some very sweary, anxious men on the hunt for alien life.

The UK Forestry Commission has marked the site with a monument to the 1980 UFO sighting. The black, galvanized-steel sculpture of the spacecraft is based on drawings supplied by the security guards who claimed to have seen it and sits at the heart of a "UFO Trail" that leads visitors through Rendlesham Forest to the spot where it all happened.

OTHERWORLDLY SCHOOL VISIT

In September 1994, children in a schoolyard in Ruwa, 64 km (40 miles) north-east of Harare in Zimbabwe, claimed to have seen a large spacecraft and several smaller UFOs land next to their school.

Alarmingly, the children were able to describe in detail the creatures that stepped out of the UFO. They talked of their large heads, long black hair, two holes for nostrils and a slit for a mouth, while some children said the beings had no mouth at all.

They claimed the creatures were dressed in dark, all-in-one suits and one child said one of them had communicated with her. She said she had a bad feeling and that the visit meant something was going to happen, that perhaps the world was going to end and that was what the creatures were trying to tell them. When asked how she was told this, she said she didn't know, but it had "popped up in her head". The creature hadn't spoken but had instead "talked with just its eyes".

THE WOOLPIT CHILDREN

One of the earlier stories of an extraterrestrial encounter harks back to the twelfth century – and also occurred in the UK county of Suffolk, a veritable hotbed of paranormal activity over the years.

Two children, claiming to be brother and sister, appeared one day in the village of Woolpit. None of the villagers had come across these children before and they looked quite different to the other children who lived there. Their skin was green in colour and they wore clothes that were unfamiliar to the time. On top of that, the children spoke in an unknown language and refused food for several days until they were offered raw broad beans, which they consumed voraciously.

The children eventually adapted to a more balanced diet and their skin lost its green hue. They were welcomed by the village, taken in by one of its residents and eventually baptized. Shortly after their baptism the boy, the younger of the two, grew ill and died.

The girl, who the villagers named Agnes, went on to learn English and told stories of their heritage, claiming they came from a land of constant twilight where the sun never shone. She referred to it as St Martin's Land.

Agnes grew up and worked for many years as a servant in the house of the villager who had taken her in. Detail is scant as to what happened to her, but some claim she went on to marry a royal official. There are even reports of Agnes' descendants still living in the village of Woolpit.

There are many theories and variations to the story of the green children of Woolpit. One astronomer hypothesized the children had been accidentally sent to Earth by way of a "matter transmitter malfunction" and explained the constant twilight as a product of the planet being trapped in a synchronous orbit. The consumption of genetically modified plants grown on their home planet was the explanation for their green skin colour, which disappeared once they began to regularly consume more earthly foods. Others suppose the children "fell from Heaven" and the general feeling was certainly that they were other worldly.

CAT AND MOUSE OVER MELBOURNE

In 1966, in Melbourne, Australia, more than 300 schoolchildren, teachers and staff witnessed multiple UFOs land in a nearby field. The craft allegedly moved silently across the sky before resting close to the schoolyard.

Conspiracy theorists believe the details of the encounter have been kept under wraps for years, possibly due to the crafts being part of a government testing programme.

One child ran into the school shouting that there was a "flying saucer" outside. The child was insistent, so other pupils and some staff members trickled outside to take a look.

The eyewitnesses claimed to have seen a round, silver object, as big as a car, with a metal antenna hovering close to the power lines. What they saw next was extraordinary – five planes surrounded the UFO and edged closer. If they got too close to the craft, it would accelerate and move in the opposite direction, then abruptly stop. When the planes attempted to approach it again, the same thing would happen – much like a game of airborne cat and mouse. This went on for around 20 minutes as the spectators watched in awe.

Then, without warning, the UFO sped away and vanished. The children were sent back to class and allegedly later warned not to speak of what they had seen or they would be punished, and staff were told they would lose their jobs if they did not keep quiet.

NORDIC SHOWDOWN

In February 1971, a small, fjord-side town in central Finland became an alleged hotspot for alien activity – with multiple encounters reported in just a few days.

One evening two women were driving down a quiet road when they saw a strange light appear behind them. The light moved over the top of their car, on to the opposite side of the road and proceeded to keep pace with them as they drove. One of the women claimed her ears felt blocked temporarily as the light passed over the vehicle.

The light eventually disappeared, but upon driving past a field a little way down the road the women saw a helmeted creature wearing a green-brown suit and standing at around 90 cm (3 ft) tall. This creature proceeded to bound across the road in front of them and vanish into the undergrowth.

Three days later, in a snowy forest nearby, two lumberjacks had spent the day hard at work and were just about to call it a day – the sky had grown dark and the light was becoming too poor to continue. One of the men had turned off his chainsaw and spied what he claimed to be a spacecraft hovering on the tree line. He described two saucers on top of each other, each around 4.5 m (15 ft) in diameter, with four spindly landing rods with rounded bases, lowering itself down to the forest floor, a portal of light emanating from the bottom of the craft. All the while his tree-felling companion remained oblivious as his chainsaw was still running.

The lumberjack stared open-mouthed as a being clad in a green suit and short in stature descended from the portal, sporting what he likened to a scuba diver's helmet. The being appeared to float down to the snowy ground, but rather than sink into it, it floated across it and toward the lumberjack.

The being promptly gathered speed and continued to move toward him in something of a robotic, anti-gravity, bounding motion. When it was 9 m (30 ft) away, in a moment of courageous bravery the lumberjack charged toward it, causing it to spin around and head back in the direction of the craft. At this point the other lumberjack who had until now been unaware of the bizarre and unbelievable scene playing out behind his back, turned around to see his workmate pelting after a small green creature, seemingly bounding across the surface of the snow.

As the brave lumberjack neared the spacecraft he saw other figures through the portal and as the bounding being began to levitate he propelled himself forward and grabbed it by the boot. He later described the sensation as he took hold of it as a searing, scalding pain as if he had wrapped his fingers around an iron fresh from the fire. According to those close to the lumberjack, the burns he sustained were still visible several months later.

As the lumberjack fell back to the ground, the being glided back into the portal, which immediately closed and the craft rose and swiftly disappeared into the sky. All that was left behind were the circular marks in the snow from the craft's landing rods.

DOUGHNUTS IN THE SKY

In 1947, a pilot flying over Puget Sound in Washington state, USA, claimed to see a strange formation in the sky ahead. Startlingly, he allegedly saw a string of nine shiny spacecraft whizzing past nearby Mount Rainier at high speed.

Reports from the ground were a little different, speaking of six "very large doughnut-shaped aircraft", one of which began "spewing forth what seemed like thousands of newspapers", which fluttered down to the ground. These "newspapers" actually turned out to be pieces of very lightweight white metal.

The sightings received news coverage across the country, with the press quickly adopting the term "flying saucer" and the two witnesses garnering much attention – some of it quite unwanted. The morning after their encounter, they claimed to have been visited by a so-called "man in black", who had been able to recount in specific detail what they had witnessed and warned them not to speak further of the incident or bad things would happen.

The sightings were later ruled to be a hoax, discredited and widely accepted to have been entirely fabricated by the two men. However, they later spoke of deciding it was easier to confess – falsely – to having made the whole thing up rather than losing sleep over further potential visits and threats from the sinister man in black.

PLAYGROUND PARANOIA

In the summer of 1977, the town of Broad Haven in Wales was subject to multiple UFO sightings – the most astonishing of which was witnessed by a group of schoolchildren.

From the playground at Broad Haven Primary School, the children spotted something unusual hovering above the neighbouring playing field. They described a "cigar-shaped" craft, with a "dome covering the middle third". The children also claimed they had seen a figure wearing a silver suit aboard the craft.

One pupil recounted hearing rumours abuzz in the classroom concerning a flying saucer outside and raced into the playground at the sound of the bell to see for himself. He described staring in wonder at the craft, which appeared for a few seconds before disappearing behind a tree, although he also admitted feeling a "strange desire to run away".

Many of the children eagerly recounted their sightings to the teachers, who were naturally sceptical. The teachers decided the most sensible course of action was to split the children up and question them separately. They were each asked to draw what they had seen and the results were nothing short of remarkable. The children all drew the same spacecraft.

There were further reports of UFO activity that same day witnessed by children in a school 11 km (7 miles) away. And some two months later, a woman residing in the next town witnessed what she described as an "upside-down saucer" aboard which were two "faceless humanoid" creatures with pointed heads. She claimed that light shone out of the craft, along with "flames of all colours", and that it gave off so much heat she felt as if her face was burning.

Many have tried to explain the events of that summer day in the Broad Haven playground, but despite the various theories not one of the schoolchildren has come forward to say they made it up. As someone with a keen interest in the case pointed out, "One child can lie, but can a whole class?"

COLD WAR LIGHT SHOW

In September 1977, while the USSR was in the throes of the Cold War with the US and its allies, in the early hours of the morning the citizens of Petrozavodsk in north-west Russia were treated to a spectacular light show.

Witnesses recounted a luminescent object that filled the night sky with light, raining down beams of light to take the form of a jellyfish. Many who saw the display were terrified and immediately took cover, believing they were under attack and that the unusual lights were in fact the fallout of the much-dreaded nuclear apocalypse. Some residents reported coin-sized holes appearing in their windowpanes following the incident.

Remarkably, UFO sightings were reported from various locations in Europe that same night in a similar time window. Residents claimed to have seen strange glowing lights over multiple Russian cities, as well as those in Lithuania and Finland. The light show in Petrozavodsk, however, was the most dramatic.

While officials put the Petrozavodsk display down to the atmospheric effects of a satellite launch, others were quick to defend what they had seen and noted that the UFO light show had travelled in a westerly direction, whereas the satellites were always launched to the east. The fact that the reports of strange activity that night were so widespread only reinforced the believers' argument that many had in fact witnessed extraterrestrial activity.

LIGHTS OVER AURORA

In 1897, 50 years before Roswell took the world by storm, a UFO was spotted flying over a farm in Aurora, Texas. The owner of the farm was a local judge and, up early that morning, he watched in awe as a disc-shaped object made its way across the sky, before descending, clipping the sail of a windmill on his land and crashing to the ground.

The pilot of the UFO died in the crash and, upon investigation, was deemed to be "not of this world". He was buried in the Aurora cemetery – a gravestone was originally placed on his grave to mark it, but this has since been removed.

Rumours were rife that the pilot was in fact a Martian, the spacecraft had featured hieroglyphics etched into its outer casing and that the crash wreckage was hidden in a well on the judge's property. In 1935, the new owner of the judge's farm claimed to have become unwell and blamed the debris in the well for contaminating his water supply. He cleared out the supposed wreckage and boarded up the water source, later building on top of it. An investigation in the 2000s that saw the well water analyzed found it was normal apart from the detection of large amounts of aluminium.

An investigation carried out by the Mutual UFO Network (MUFON) in the 1970s uncovered two new eyewitnesses to the crash. One, who was 15 at the time, spoke of how her parents went to the crash site (she was not allowed to go) and claimed to have seen the alien body for themselves. Another, who was ten at the time, recalled seeing the craft trailing smoke across the sky. He also remembered how his father had gone into town the next day and returned with tales of seeing part of the wreckage from the crash.

The same investigation saw MUFON explore the Aurora cemetery with a metal detector, looking for signs of the supposed alien grave. They allegedly uncovered a small, flying saucer-shaped marker and picked up readings from the metal detector over the grave. However, upon asking for permission to exhume what lay beneath they were denied. Upon returning to the grave site, MUFON found the marker had been removed and their metal detector no longer received readings as it had before. Had the contents of the grave been removed?

The Aurora incident remains shrouded in mystery and something of a favourite among UFO enthusiasts. It has been subject to countless investigations and documentaries, and saw the release of dedicated feature film *The Aurora Encounter* in 1986.

ANCIENT ALIEN ENCOUNTERS

As far back as in Palaeolithic and Neolithic cave paintings there is evidence of humans glimpsing objects in the sky that they didn't understand. However, it was in Roman times that the documentation of such events became more formal.

Considered the first written mention of a UFO sighting, in 218 BC the historian Livy wrote about "phantom ships seen gleaming in the sky", however modern historians and ufologists are torn over whether his writings were literal or metaphorical.

In 74 BC, the biographer and essayist Plutarch described some very unusual aerial activity above a battlefield, writing:

With no apparent change of weather, the sky burst asunder and a huge, flame-like body was seen to fall between the two armies. In shape it was most like a wine-jar, and in colour like molten silver.

The flaming UFO was witnessed by thousands on the battlefield, including the king himself.

In the first century AD ancient scholar Titus Flavius Josephus witnessed something so unbelievable he felt the need to apologize for relaying it, thinking all who heard the tale would consider it a fable, as he explained he had seen "chariots and armed battalions hurtling through the clouds and encompassing the cities".

Some ufologists believe otherworldly beings visited ancient communities and advised them on how to build cities or successfully grow crops, theorizing that these alien beings were often interpreted as gods by those with whom they communicated.

MYSTERY MALADY ON FALCON LAKE

In May of 1967, in Manitoba, Canada, a local man was prospecting for silver ore on the shores of Falcon Lake. He saw two glowing objects hovering in the distance and watched while one flew away and the other landed some 46 m (150 ft) away from where he was standing. He claimed the object was a silver craft, around 11 m (35 ft) in diameter, smooth with no seams and brilliantly lit.

His curiosity getting the better of him, the man approached the craft and was close enough to peer into the doorway. Inside, he reported seeing light beams and panels with lights flashing in different colours, but no beings. He reached out to touch the craft and it was so hot it melted the fingertips of his gloves. Without warning, three panels slid across the doorway and the craft lifted off suddenly. It began to spin around and he noticed a panel with a grid of holes. A blast through the panel struck him in the chest and knocked him to the ground, setting his shirt on fire. He struggled out of his clothes and stumbled through the woods to his motel where he caught a bus to hospital.

Photographs of his body in hospital show burn marks in a grid of dots on his chest and stomach, with similar patterns burned into the shirt he was wearing that night. His nine-year-old son later described his visit to his father's bedside and recalled a strong smell of "sulphur and burnt motor", adding "it was all around and it was coming out of his pores". Over the next few weeks, the man grew ill and suffered from excruciating headaches, nausea and blackouts, along with other symptoms similar to radiation sickness. His sickness lasted many months and the burn marks on his chest and stomach would heal only to reappear again.

The Falcon Lake incident is one of the most documented UFO sightings in Canada and is widely considered by believers to be a true extraterrestrial encounter. Several books have been written about the incident and in 2018 the Canadian Mint released a limited-edition commemorative $20 coin to recognize the event.

THE JAPAN AIRLINES SPOOKY ESCORT

In November 1986, Japan Airlines flight 1628 was en route from Paris to Tokyo when, just after sunset, it encountered two UFOs in the sky above eastern Alaska. The objects swiftly rose from below the plane and closed in on the aircraft, appearing to escort it. Each of the UFOs featured a square grid of glowing light, thought to be some kind of engine thrusters, which were dazzlingly bright and the crew reported how the aircraft cabin lit up when it was close to the craft. The captain even claimed he could feel the heat on his face.

Recalling the event, the captain said he had at first assumed the objects were military planes, but when they attempted to match the speed of the aircraft from a sideways approach he described them as appearing to defy gravity. He explained how the objects sped up, then stopped, then flew at exactly the same speed as the aircraft and in the same direction, before changing course the next instant.

Eventually the UFOs moved away from the plane and a third, much larger, disc-shaped craft started following them. As the light of a city below lit up the third craft, its true size became apparent and the captain described it as being twice the size of an aircraft carrier with a pale band of light around its middle. The smaller UFOs had been picked up by air traffic control, which requested confirmation of the objects showing up on their radar – but none of the pilots who responded could identify the strange air traffic. A military craft was deployed around half an hour later, but it was only able to distinguish Japan Airlines flight 1628 – the UFOs were no longer present.

TASMANIAN PURSUIT

In October 1978, a young Australian pilot was flying over the Bass Strait toward Tasmania's King Island, with a plan to land there and catch crayfish.

However, at around 7 p.m. something crossed the sky above him at a terrific speed. He was startled, to say the least, and curious as to what it could be. He radioed air traffic control to ask if there were any known aircraft in the area, but was informed there were not.

The young pilot described over the radio what he had seen – a long, metallic object, with a green light and what he surmised to be four bright landing lights – pass at least 1,000 feet above him. He grew nervous and told the controller the craft seemed to be playing some sort of game with him, by now having flown over two or three times at great speed. The object then vanished before reappearing on the other side of his aircraft.

The controller kept the young pilot talking in an attempt to reassure him and garner as much information as possible. Then came the pilot's words: "It is hovering and it is not an aircraft." The radio fell silent for 17 seconds before it cut out.

Those were the final words of the pilot. After the transmission cut out he was never seen or heard from again. Nor was his aircraft ever recovered. An extensive search of the water and surrounding land was conducted, but no trace of him or his plane – nor any evidence of a crash site – were found.

The pilot's disappearance was reported worldwide, with many concluding he had been abducted by extraterrestrial beings. The plot thickened when it was discovered he had neglected to inform the King Island airport of his intention to land and that he was in fact a UFO obsessive. The pilot's father remained convinced his son was still alive and had been taken by the UFO and released elsewhere, far away.

ALIEN ASSAULT

In 1979, a Scottish forestry worker saw something unusual in the woods that made headlines around the world.

The man had been carrying out his regular duties in the forest that day, when he came across what he could only describe as a spaceship in a clearing. He described it as being 9 m (30 ft) high and dome-shaped, explaining how two spiked spheres dropped from the craft and rolled along the ground toward him.

He fell to the ground and as he was starting to lose consciousness, he felt aware of something grabbing his legs and could smell burning. He woke up feeling nauseous about 20 minutes later, his trousers ripped in several places. The clearing was now empty, the craft gone, but he saw strange marks in the ground where it once stood.

Feeling dazed as he got into his car, he managed to drive into a ditch. He got out of the car, stumbled home and his wife called the police. They treated his ripped clothing and minor injuries seriously as one of the more unusual cases of their career – assault by aliens.

The man was a pillar of the community, a respected war hero, teetotaller and avid churchgoer. He was well-liked and no one had any reason to doubt he believed he had seen something.

He never wavered from his version of events and swore by every detail for the rest of his life.

The police were baffled by the marks on the forest floor. They could see something that weighed several tonnes had stood there for a time, but there was no indication it had been dragged or driven away. It could only have flown or been lifted into the air.

Ufologists agree this to be one of the few cases in the world that utterly defy explanation.

TIME TRAVEL AND ALTERNATE REALITIES

It's time to delve into the possibilities of time travel and the multiverse – the multiple parallel universes and realities operating potentially side by side.

Some have claimed to travel back and forth through time on specific missions, in some cases purporting to have saved the world. Others have said they have visited pivotal moments throughout history.

Then there are those who without intention have found themselves experiencing a time-slip, travelling from one era to another with no idea how. The burning question: do they ever make it home?

We look at stories of people who believe they've experienced a "glitch in the matrix", either crossing over from one reality into an alternate one – briefly or forever – or interacting with ghostly echoes of those people who have crossed the vortex.

And don't forget doppelgängers – we tell the stories of those who have met their doubles from alternate realities or experienced dramatic life events because of them. What would you do if you met yourself?

TIME TUNNEL

The Bermuda Triangle is famous for mysterious disappearances of boats and planes, but one man who flew through it lived to tell the tale of his mysterious encounter.

In 1970, a man was flying his six-seater plane from the Bahamas to Florida, with his father and business partner on board. The flight path would take them through the Bermuda Triangle, but they had flown through it many times before and weren't superstitious.

On the journey, the plane became engulfed in a strange cloud that seemed to be mirroring the plane's movements and was difficult to shake. They broke out of the cloud, only to fly straight into another, similarly unusual one straight ahead. This cloud appeared white and fluffy from the outside, a regular, safe, standard cloud, as far as they were concerned. Once on the inside, however, it was dark and flashes of light led them to believe they had found themselves in the middle of an electrical storm.

The pilot turned the plane at this point, to try to break free of the storm, and radioed air traffic control to notify them of the plane's change of course. He realized the first cloud had clearly fused with the second to form a sort of cloud tunnel. Try as he might, he couldn't break out and, as he could see blue sky up ahead – albeit several miles ahead – he decided the best course of action was to press on ahead and power through the tunnel.

Inside this strange misty tube, the pilot described some very strange occurrences indeed. He claimed there to have been spiralling lines swirling in a counter-clockwise motion and that as the plane moved forward the tunnel was shrinking in diameter and length. What at first had appeared to a trained pilot's eye to be a 6 km (10 mile) long tunnel, which he estimated would take around three minutes to pass through, had become a length of only one mile and took them all of 20 seconds.

At the end of the tunnel, the passengers described feeling weightless for around 10 seconds before being plunged into a strange grey haze all around them that engulfed the plane. They attempted to read their location via the plane's navigation system, but it was malfunctioning so they radioed air traffic control once again. Confused, air traffic control replied that they couldn't see any planes at all on the flight path the pilot claimed they were following.

The grey haze began to clear in what the pilot described as ribbons of fog across the sky and the controller radioed the plane to announce he could see them heading into Miami. The pilot was baffled – the plane had only been in the air for around 30 minutes and he knew this journey well, it should have taken much longer.

He saw Miami up ahead, confirming the controller's observation, and prepared for landing. Once the plane was safely on the ground the journey time was noted at 48 minutes – but the fastest the pilot had ever managed this flight was 75 minutes. To this day, he insists they must have flown into some kind of time warp high up over the ocean.

PREDICTIONS FROM THE FUTURE

In 2000, a man started posting on myriad internet message boards claiming to be from the year 2036 and on a mission to, effectively, save the world. He told anyone who would listen that in 2036 a computer virus had wiped out "everything" and he was on his way to 1975 in order to retrieve an IBM 5100 computer, which apparently had vital parts to help fight the bug. He explained the purpose of his stop-off in 2000 to be for personal reasons – he wanted to visit his family and collect lost photographs.

For around four months the time traveller responded to any questions posed to him about the future via these message boards, relaying information about the future – or a possible future – and sending warnings to those who interacted with him.

He urged everyone to prioritize learning first aid and warned people against eating beef, claiming that mad cow disease and CJD were rife in his future reality. He claimed a second US Civil War had divided the country into five regions and that the new capital of the USA was in Omaha, Nebraska. He also told of a Third World War kicking off in 2015, started by

Russia and involving a nuclear exchange with the US. This, he said, resulted in the deaths of three billion people.

The man described his time machine and the process of time travel in technical language, saying the machine was a "stationary mass, temporal displacement unit powered by two top-spin, dual-positive singularities", which produced a "standard offset Tipler sinusoid". It also featured a cooling and X-ray venting system, gravity sensors, four caesium clocks and three computer units. All of this was housed in a 1987 Chevrolet.

In early 2001, the man made his final post, advising people to always "bring a gas can with you when the car dies on the side of the road". He claimed he was leaving this time period and heading home to 2036 via 1975 – and he was never heard from again.

Many of these predictions have not come to fruition, but there are people who believe the man was from an alternate future, the path from the past world to his future altered somehow along the way.

A STEP BACK IN VERSAILLES

On August 10, 1911, two British women visiting the Palace of Versailles outside Paris claimed to have stepped back in time to revolutionary France.

The women grew bored of their organized tour and wandered off through the stunning palace gardens and up to the Grand Trianon park, which houses Petit Trianon, a small manor house in the palace grounds, which was built in the 1760s during Louis XV's reign and later given to Queen Marie Antoinette by her husband Louis XVI.

In 1911, the park gates were closed so the women tourists decided to try another route, using their map, but they got lost and ended up walking down an alleyway that led somewhere else altogether. The women described experiencing a physical feeling of great oppression. They witnessed several people, all wearing garments that seemed old-fashioned to them, including cloaks and three-cornered hats. They also briefly interacted with a blonde woman wearing a dress from a bygone age as she sketched on the grass.

They also claimed to have experienced scenes that felt "unnatural" and "unpleasant". They passed a cottage where a woman was passing a jug to a girl in the doorway – they described this scene as being frozen, as if the people were in fact waxworks. They also spoke of the trees becoming "flat and lifeless, like wood worked in tapestry". One of them added that "there were no effects of light and shade, and no wind stirred the trees".

The women returned to the palace and were directed to rejoin the tour from which they had wandered off, which they duly did. They didn't speak of this incident for a week, but after that regrouped and decided they should each write down their own version of events and compare.

Upon completion of their accounts, they discussed the events and pondered over the possible haunting of the area around the Palace of Versailles. They later came to the conclusion that they may well have visited August 10, 1792 – six weeks before the abolition of the French monarchy. They also believed that the blonde woman sketching on the grass may well have been Marie Antoinette.

The women returned to the Grand Trianon several times in an attempt to trace their footsteps and see the past once again, but to no avail. Ten years later, under pen names, the women published the book *An Adventure* about their experiences. The book caused a sensation, although few felt able to take it particularly seriously.

DON'T FORGET THE KITCHEN SINK

In 2006, a Swedish man claimed to have travelled into the future and interacted with his future self – and he had evidence for it.

While fixing a leak under his kitchen sink, the man reached up and realized the space he was occupying was expanding. He continued to reach up until he saw a light and was able to stand upright. Suddenly he found himself outside and face to face with an older version of himself.

The year was 2042 and he was in his 70s. The man quizzed his older self to confirm his suspicions were true and, lo and behold, he knew his secrets and personal stories. They both had the same tattoo on their forearm, although his older self's tattoo was rather faded. The two laughed and joked with each other as if they were old friends.

The younger time traveller took several photographs and filmed the two of them laughing and catching up with each other. When critics dismissed his claims of travelling into the future he simply said: "I met myself there in the future and had a great time. I don't really care what other people think."

GETAWAYS TO GETTYSBURG

An attorney from Seattle, Washington, USA has made several claims that he participated in a secret time-travelling programme led by the US government, which started when he was seven years old and came to an end when he was twelve.

The man alleges the experiment – named Project Pegasus and led by government agency DARPA (Defense Advanced Research Projects Agency) – began in the 1970s and saw children teleported into both the past and future. The programme used children in its experiments because it claimed they could adapt well to "the strains of moving between past, present and future".

The project allegedly utilized several different types of time-travel technology – the man claims to have travelled via eight different routes – most of which involved a teleporter which was built using the specifics from technical papers found in Nikola Tesla's apartment following his death.

The man claimed to have teleported at least five times to Ford's Theatre in Washington DC on the night of Abraham Lincoln's assassination, as well as to Gettysburg – the site of the eponymous address delivered by President Lincoln during the American Civil War – where he was allegedly photographed.

He said each of his visits to the past were different, even if they involved going back to the same time and place. He believed that the programme was sending the children to "slightly different alternative realities on adjacent timelines". As he travelled more and more, he alleges to have bumped into himself during two different visits. On trips to Gettysburg he was armed with a letter that would explain the situation to the Navy secretary, should he be arrested for suspicious doppelgänger behaviour.

The man also claimed that in the future – some time between 2016 and 2028 – he had visited realities where he was either president or vice president of the USA. He ran for president in 2016, but, as we all know only too well, someone else won that year.

SHIFTING THROUGH A VORTEX

In recent times, a woman from California, USA, purported to have moved through a vortex, possibly via some form of astral projection. She was in her car waiting in traffic one day when the street "waved" in front of her, forming – briefly – a curving S-shape.

The woman blinked several times, but sure enough, she knew what she had seen. However, she decided it must have simply been an optical illusion and so she drove home.

Upon arriving at home, she found her daughter shaking and unable to speak. Her daughter eventually composed herself and was able to tell her mother that she had just seen her walk through the door and go into the bathroom just a few minutes earlier.

The woman claimed to believe she had likely travelled from one dimension to another – from one reality to another – "Either that, or the other me didn't want to come out and face me," she said.

SEEING DOUBLE

The idea of döppelgangers is rooted firmly in legend. Many people believe they have a double of themselves somewhere in the world, living their parallel life; others believe them to be an echo of themselves crossing over into – or existing in – another reality.

Throughout history people believed the sight of their doppelgänger meant their own death was imminent. Queen Elizabeth I of England claimed to have seen her own dead body not long before she died and poet Percy Shelley – married to Mary of Frankenstein fame – said he was visited by a phantom of himself who led him to the seashore and pointed out to sea. He died in a sailing accident shortly afterward.

In the past doppelgängers were viewed by mystics as a type of shape-shifting demon, but these days, people prefer to think of them as harmless reflections of ourselves in a different reality or time phase. Many believe there are multiple versions of ourselves existing at all times in multiple realities and when we spot a doppelgänger it is in fact because we have the ability to move from one time phase to another – but this is easier for some people to achieve than others.

Some scientific theories concerning doppelgängers claim that these are in fact "tricks of the mind", hallucinations or visions experienced by those with mental heath issues or impaired brain function.

One anecdote that doesn't fit this theory, however, due in no small part to the sheer number of witnesses, is that of French schoolteacher Emilie Sagée. In 1845 she was working in a Latvian French-language girls' school, she excelled in her role and was liked by both pupils and colleagues. However, things took a turn when Sagée's doppelgänger appeared in front of her class as she was writing on the blackboard. The double began to mimic Sagée's actions. On another occasion her double appeared as she was eating a meal in the crowded dining hall, again mimicking her movements.

Sagée could not see her own double, but according to reports the original Sagée would grow pale and appear fatigued whenever her doppelgänger was sighted.

One day Sagée was picking flowers in the school garden when a class of pupils claimed she had appeared in front of them out of nowhere and stared straight at them in a cold and menacing fashion. The pupils had been in the middle of a sewing class when their teacher stepped out of the room for a moment; Sagée's double had materialized from thin air and frightened them all.

Sagée was eventually sacked from her job because her doppelgänger was causing too many disturbances and frightening the bejesus out of everyone at the school.

THE MAN FROM TAURED

In 1954, a man arrived at Haneda Airport in Tokyo, Japan, from a European flight. As he made his way through customs, he politely answered the officials' questions. He was travelling to Japan on business, as he had already had on two other occasions that year. He was able to converse in Japanese, but his mother tongue was French.

All sounds relatively normal, but things took a turn when he told them his country of origin. The man stated he was from Taured and the officials looked at him with blank expressions. Taured does not exist, they told him. The man assured them it did exist – on the border between France and Spain – and showed them his passport. Sure enough, his passport appeared to be for a citizen of a nation called Taured (which of course does not exist) and the pages showed various visa stamps including two for entry to Japan.

The officials called the company the man claimed he was doing business with, but they had no prior knowledge of him; they called the hotel he claimed he was staying at, but they had no record of a booking in his name; they looked at his chequebook and it featured the name of a bank that did not exist.

The man began to grow irate – what was wrong with these people? He had sailed through customs on the previous two occasions, but this time all the staff seemed to be ignorant about the countries of the world and claimed to not know of his home nation. The officials showed him a map of Europe and pointed to Andorra – was this where the man was from? No! He insisted he was from Taured and claimed his home country had a history dating back more than 1,000 years.

The man was escorted to a hotel where they found a room for him. Due to the mysterious circumstances his room was guarded by immigration officers and his identity documents held by airport officials.

The next morning, the hotel room was empty and the man was gone. Everyone was baffled – his room had been guarded all night – and the mystery deepened further when his passport and driving licence disappeared from the airport security office.

Theories suggest the man from Taured had crossed over into an alternate reality and had managed to cross back that night. Whatever happened, we can only hope he made his way safely home.

GLITCH IN THE MATRIX

A young hostess at a bar/restaurant in Colorado claimed to have seated a couple at their table – but before they even arrived.

She described greeting the man and woman at the door who asked if they could sit outside. She distinctly remembered them because the woman wore a necklace with a large, striking jewel and she complimented her on it. They exchanged pleasantries as the hostess walked them through the restaurant to a table outside and handed them their menus. Then she returned to them with two glasses of water and told them a member of waiting staff would be with them shortly to take their order.

Some five minutes later the same couple arrived at the door of the restaurant. The hostess said, "Hello, again!" and asked if they needed to be re-seated. They looked confused and asked for a table for two outside. The hostess again clocked the striking jewel around the woman's neck. Confused, she walked them through the restaurant to the same table and found it empty apart from the menus and two glasses of water. She quickly removed the glasses and promised to return with two more.

Looking flummoxed at the bar as she poured the water, one of the waitresses asked if she was OK, saying she had seen her walking through the restaurant talking to herself clutching menus and had then seen her set the menus on the outside table as if there were people sitting there, but the chairs had been empty. She then saw her pour two glasses of water and take them over to the empty table. The hostess was even more flummoxed at this point and asked the waitress if she could see people seated at the table now. Then it was the waitress' turn to look confused and she said, "Of course."

TIME SLIP ON HIGH

In 1935, a British RAF pilot was flying over Scotland on his way from Andover in England to Edinburgh. He looked down as he passed over Drem and the abandoned, dilapidated airfield there, taking it all in from a great height. The airfield had been left to ruin a long time ago, now overgrown with greenery that even the cows were wandering through.

A couple of days later he was making his return journey from Edinburgh to Andover when his plane hit a storm. Along with high winds and heavy rain, there were threatening clouds, but the odd thing about them was they were yellow and seemed to go on forever.

It was turbulent and the pilot began to lose control of the plane. It began to drop, but then broke through the clouds into bright and sunny skies, with no sign of yellow storm clouds. He barely had time to consider how strange a weather experience he had encountered when he caught sight of the Drem airfield, no longer overgrown with cattle roaming, it appeared to be a fully functioning airbase with several yellow planes sat on the runway. He was close enough to see the staff at the airfield in their blue overalls – which was odd because RAF mechanics wore brown overalls in 1935 – and more curious still was the fact that there were no yellow planes functioning in the RAF.

He also spotted an unusual type of monoplane he had never seen before.

Having only just regained control of the plane, the storm appeared to descend once more and the plane was again engulfed in strange yellow clouds. Despite the fierce nature of the storm, as before, it didn't last long and the plane was released into sunny skies with the storm nowhere to be seen.

The pilot went on to safely land the plane and told his fellow pilots of his experience. Of course, most didn't believe him so he kept quiet. However, by 1939 the Drem airfield was up and running again, the RAF had started painting their training aeroplanes yellow and the mechanics' overalls had been swapped from brown to blue.

The pilot could only surmise he had somehow travelled into the future, albeit briefly, via the yellow storm clouds.

LONG LIVE
THE BEATLES

In 2009, a man from California made an extraordinary claim about The Beatles. He had been driving home with his dog one day, when he had to stop to let her do her business by the roadside. Once she had finished she got distracted by a rabbit and bounded after it. He ran after her, but tripped and managed to knock himself out.

When he came around he found himself propped up next to a strange machine he had never seen before and there was a man there. The stranger introduced himself and said he had found the man's unconscious body while on a business trip for an interdimensional travel agency.

The two men conversed about their different worlds, both equally as interested in the world the other hailed from. They ended up chatting about music, which is when the interdimensional traveller said in his world The Beatles were all still alive and still making music – they had never split up. He produced a cassette tape which he let the man keep – supposedly an album that did not exist in our world called *Everyday Chemistry*, featuring songs he had never heard before.

TIME TRAVEL AND ALTERNATE REALITIES

The traveller bade the man farewell and they parted company. He set up the website thebeatlesneverbrokeup.com and uploaded the songs alleged to not exist in this dimension, so you can decide for yourself what you think of this!

WAKING UP IN A PARALLEL UNIVERSE

In 2008, a Spanish woman in her 40s claimed she had woken up in a different world. Her surroundings looked very similar to the one she knew and had fallen asleep in, but there were striking discrepancies.

In the reality that she knew, she had split up with her long-term boyfriend six months previously and had started a new relationship. Things were going well, they had been together for four months and she had even met his son. Yet in this new reality she was still living with her ex-boyfriend, who seemed to believe they were still together, and she could find no trace of her new boyfriend or his son.

She went to work, but some of the staff were people she had never seen before. She approached her office only to find it occupied with a different name on the door. Confused, she connected her laptop to the office Wi-Fi and found herself on the company network – she did still work for the company, but in a completely different department and with different people.

She took the day off, needing some space to process what was happening, and went straight to the doctor. They ran some tests and concluded she hadn't been drugged. She wondered if she had experienced a nervous breakdown and dreamt the new relationship and career changes. Or perhaps she had suffered from amnesia and forgotten the past six months. She had no explanation. She underwent further medical tests, but they found nothing to be awry either physically or mentally.

She hired a private investigator to find her new boyfriend and his son, but to no avail. The investigator could find no trace of him and said it was as if he didn't exist.

She asked her sister how her shoulder was holding up following her operation – family members looked at her strangely, her sister had never had any problems with her shoulder and certainly hadn't undergone any surgery.

As the days, weeks and months went by, she learned more and more about the differences between her new life and the old one. The woman had to accept that this was her new reality. The only explanation she could come up with for her predicament was that she had crossed over into a parallel universe.

PARALLEL EARTH

In 1972, in Utah, USA, four women were heading home after a road trip when they took a wrong turn.

They had been driving along on black asphalt roads through the desert, but when they took the turning found themselves in an immediately different environment. No longer arid desert, they drove across white cement roads surrounded by grain fields and lakes.

Up ahead they saw a building with a huge neon sign, but it appeared to be written in a language and alphabet they were unfamiliar with. They pulled up, hoping to get some help with directions, when a large group of very tall men exited the building waving their arms furiously.

The women realized to their horror that these men did not appear to be human and so stepped on the gas and motored back the way they had come. As they fled they realized they were being followed – four strange egg-shaped vehicles each mounted on three spindly wheels were following them. The women sped up and managed to lose the strange creatures.

They drove back to the desert canyon and normality appeared to be restored, so they made their way home. The only explanation they could suggest for what had happened was that they had somehow crossed over to a parallel Earth, or perhaps jumped to a different time.

MANDELA EFFECT

The term "Mandela effect" was coined to refer to a type of collective misremembering. Great swathes of people will be convinced that they remember a common event or detail a certain way, only to discover that their memories were somehow falsely implanted and that they've remembered it all wrong.

The phenomenon gets its name from a common misconception that South African ex-president Nelson Mandela had died in prison in the 1980s. Some people even claimed they remembered watching clips of his funeral on television. In actual fact, Mandela was freed from prison in 1990, went on to serve as South African president from 1994 until 1999 and only died in 2013.

Paranormal experts ascribe this collective misremembering to movement between alternate realities – the multiverse as opposed to the universe of the non-believers. Another theory suggests that these collective false memories are caused by time travellers altering history as they wade through the space-time continuum.

Other examples of the Mandela effect include: thinking the Warner Brothers cartoon show was called *Looney Toons*, when in fact it has always been called *Looney Tunes*; believing the moustachioed and top-hatted man from the Monopoly board game has a monocle, despite the fact he very much does not; swearing blind the *Mona Lisa* used to have a more obvious smile; thinking C-3PO is all gold, when in fact his right leg is silver from the knee down; believing Darth Vader never said "Luke, I am your father", all he said was "I am your father"; Americans and foreigners remembering being told the USA has 51 or 52 states – it's just 50; many people thinking astronaut Neil Armstrong was still alive, when in fact he passed away in 2012; believing Mother Theresa was made a saint back in the 1990s, when in fact it didn't happen until 2016; remembering Patrick Swayze recovering from cancer, when sadly he died in 2009; and claiming Leonardo DiCaprio won an Oscar long, long ago, when in fact he picked up his first in 2016.

Now there are a few things to think about...

REMEMBERING RIVERSIDE

In 2006, a woman was driving through San Bernadino, California, USA. She was only passing through that day, but when she saw a sign for Riverside, the town where her family had lived for generations since the early 1800s, she decided to stop off and drink in a little nostalgia, perhaps even drive past what used to be her grandmother's house where she had lived for a while after college.

She was very familiar with the town, knew where relatives' houses were and had been visiting her grandparents' graves in the cemetery for years. Rain was pouring down and her car windows were up, but the moment she decided to stop and visit her grandparents' graves she smelt a big blast of cigar smoke enter the car. Her grandfather had died when she was five, he had been a cigar smoker and that was pretty much the only thing she remembered about him. Spooked, and deterred by the rain, she decided not to stop off but instead to press on to her destination.

She returned to Riverside the next day and was confused by what she found. Nothing was particularly familiar. Her grandparents' street didn't look quite right and she couldn't find the house they had lived in. All of the houses were built in a different style and looked completely unfamiliar. Modern, ranch-style houses sat where her grandmother's Tudor home had once been.

Where the cemetery had once stood was a fenced off bit of scrubland with no graves. She was baffled. She drove around a little more, in a desperate attempt to find something she recognized. She found the city college and school, which looked as they should, but when she drove on to the main drag it was completely different.

Once housing all the restaurants, banks and hotels, what she found was a "ghetto" – an urban wasteland covered in graffiti. The woman was really quite frightened by her experience. She sat in her car for several hours, refusing to get out in case something bad might happen and she would be sucked into another reality. Finally, she plucked up the courage to drive back to her hotel – worried that wouldn't be there either and that the whole world would now be unfamiliar to her. Luckily, it wasn't.

A couple of years later the woman's father died and had requested to be buried in the cemetery in Riverside next to her grandparents. Remembering the fenced-off scrub, she panicked, but when she returned for the funeral the town was back to how she remembered it. Her father was buried in the family plot, her relatives' houses were still there, things looked a hell of a lot more familiar than they had a couple of years previously and even the main drag was back to its bright shiny self.

TIME TRAVEL TOMB

In Brompton Cemetery in London, England, the largest tomb in the grounds is rumoured to be a time machine. Brompton is one of the "Magnificent Seven" burial sites created in the nineteenth century in the capital, during an era when London was running out of space to house the dead.

The striking mausoleum stands taller than anything else in the graveyard, looming over its neighbours with a commanding presence. Built in 1854 to house a nineteenth-century heiress – and eventually two of her daughters – its exterior features several nods to Egyptology, allegedly an obsession of the inhabitant, in terms of its shape and large bronze door marking the entrance. Hieroglyphics adorn the walls, along with reproductions of some of the more obscure Leonardo da Vinci sketches that supposedly detail the secret of time travel.

The tomb itself was created collaboratively by a sculptor and eccentric Victorian inventor. However, in 1853 the inventor was mysteriously murdered and the key to the door of the mausoleum went missing, only fuelling the time-machine rumours.

Many believe the tomb is a time-travel device that offers the holder of the key teleportation opportunities and that it might even have a direct link with a graveyard in Paris.

TIMES SQUARE TIME TRAVELLER

Now known to be an urban legend spawned by a short story, the tale of the Times Square Time Traveller is nonetheless a fascinating one. In 1950, in New York City, a 30-year-old man appeared in Times Square, apparently gawking at the cars, lights and signs "like he'd never seen them before". He was sadly killed crossing a road, hit by a speeding cab because he misunderstood the traffic lights.

The man was delivered to the morgue, and his clothing and possessions were examined. He had on his person several coins in mint condition that had not been produced for several decades, as well as a bill from a livery stable and brass shotgun slug – both curious items for one to carry in 1950. He also carried a letter with a postmark of 1876 and items bearing the name Rudolph Fentz, showing his address as being on Fifth Avenue.

The investigating officer could find no evidence of anyone under that name listed in the phone directory and the residential address on his personal effects had been operating as a business for many years. The man's clothes were very old-fashioned – the style estimated to be out of date by as much as

75 years – and his suit sported a label featuring the name of a tailor no one had ever heard of, his hat the name of a store that had gone out of business a long time ago.

There were no open missing person's cases matching the man's description and his fingerprints didn't match any the police had on file. Everyone was stumped.

The police got their hands on an old phone directory and found a Rudolph Fentz Jr listed. Investigations discovered him to be a man in his 60s who had died five years previously, but the police were able to make contact with his wife who was still alive. She claimed that her father-in-law, Rudolph Fentz Sr, had gone missing in the 1870s, supposedly going out for a walk at 10 p.m. and never returning. The investigating officer managed to track down the missing person's report from 1876 only to find the photograph matched their man from Times Square.

FINAL WORD

By now you will have had enough paranormal fodder to no doubt make your pulse race, your hair follicles twitch and your fingernails ache. I hope that was spine-chilling enough for you.

The history of the paranormal is a fascinating one, the weird and bizarre often making life more interesting – at least for some of us looking back from centuries in the future. But among the strange and unusual lie the human stories and those affected along the way, for whatever reason. We honour their memory by retelling their stories.

Remember, next time you cosy up to watch a horror film featuring a horrifically angry poltergeist or other-worldly blood-baying creature; maybe a comic book charting the apocalypse with a never-ending slew of flesh-eating zombies; or a piece of classic literature dedicated to "bizzare humans" and their supposed inhuman capabilities – the ideas all had to come from somewhere.

Have you enjoyed this book?
If so, why not write a review on your favourite website?

If you're interested in finding out more about our books, find
us on Facebook at **Summersdale Publishers**, on Twitter at
@Summersdale and on Instagram at **@summersdalebooks** and
get in touch. We'd love to hear from you!

Thanks very much for buying this Summersdale book.

www.summersdale.com

CONSPIRACY THEORIES

A Compendium of History's
Greatest Mysteries and More
Recent Cover-Ups

Jamie King

ISBN: 978-1-78783-565-8

URBAN LEGENDS

Strange Tales and Unsolved
Mysteries from Around the World

James Proud

ISBN: 978-1-80007-106-3